658.5
Sch 25

Total Quality Performance

Highlights of a Conference

Edited by
Lawrence Schein
and
Melissa A. Berman

D1024515

WITHDRAWN
ST. MARYS COLLEGE LIBRARY

A Report from The Conference Board

LIBRARY ST. MARY'S COLLEGE
172104

Contents

WITHDRAWN
ST. MARYS COLLEGE LIBRARY

Editors' Acknowledgement

The editors would like to thank Frank Caropreso for his skillful help in editing these speeches.

From the President

The drive for total quality is at the top of the corporate agenda, as the success of the Board's first conference on this issue indicates.

The Conference Board has had an active program in this area since 1985, when the U.S. Quality Council was formed to provide executives leading their corporate quality processes with an opportunity to exchange ideas and experiences. This year, we launched a European Quality Council.

Efforts to develop and implement the total quality process benefit from knowing how others have managed this enormous change in culture and operations. The Conference Board is pleased to be able to contribute to that learning experience—our traditional role.

This report presents practical information on quality programs in nearly 20 firms that are leaders in the quality process. Executives directly involved in these efforts discussed the progress and pitfalls they are encountering. The Conference Board appreciates the participation of all the experts who spoke at this meeting. Their contributions offer a valuable perspective to executives in every industry.

JAMES T. MILLS
President

Introduction

This volume presents the highlights of a conference on Total Quality Performance (January 21-22, 1988), The Conference Board's first on this topic.

Intense and successful foreign competition, coupled with a huge trade deficit, has fueled a critical and often painful reappraisal of the way Americans think about work and the methods we use in generating products and services. One consequence is that quality has come front and center in the national consciousness. In 1987, Congress enacted the Baldridge National Quality Improvement Act under which the Secretary of Commerce and the National Bureau of Standards will develop and administer awards to outstanding companies. Firms in Japan and Western European countries are also deeply involved in quality programs, and many of these nations also have quality awards.

At its broadest level, the focus on quality is part of this decade's corporate restructuring to make business more competitive. At the most basic level, the effort involves economic survival. Melvin Howard, Xerox's Vice Chairman, who chaired one of the conference sessions, put the matter succinctly:

> The primary factor behind the interest in quality programs is a recognition on the part of business that it may have to make significant changes in many ways it does business, from developing and manufacturing products to marketing and servicing them. The primary reasons are cost and competition.

Another conference chairperson, Lorraine Scarpa, Vice President, Customer Information Marketing for Dun & Bradstreet, suggests the magnitude of the change:

> Corporate management is now vastly more sensitive to the need today to change corporate culture in the pursuit of quality as a lever against competition.

Quality as a mindset, a technology, and a way of managing resources is being examined as never before as a means of restoring the nation's economic health. The effort has moved from a narrow focus on product quality control and quality assurance to an organization-wide emphasis—applied to all business functions, all services and goods, all employees. In this evolution, the customer perspective has become paramount: Quality is defined and driven by customer requirements. The challenge to companies is to integrate customer needs into every phase of the business.

The companies on the conference agenda are among those on the leading edge of this movement. Despite the great variety of industry types and sizes they represent, their statements and programs reflect a common set of principles. For example:

- Productivity, particularly in white-collar work, can increase only after a major commitment is made to long-term quality improvement objectives that are shared throughout the organization. Total quality performance requires total organizational dedication and involvement, especially from top management.
- Quality requires listening intently to both internal and external customers and meeting or exceeding customer specifications by "doing the right things right the first time."
- Quality work demands understanding and "ownership" of the manufacturing and service operations. Understanding the processes requires training all employees in detecting problems and in bringing deviations under ever-tightening tolerances.
- The cost of quality, that is, the cost of poor work, is 20 percent to 30 percent of revenues. A key to cost reduction is creating error-free design before manufacturing and before service delivery even occurs.

The presentations in this report explain how companies are applying these principles to their specific competitive situations.

- To provide a broad perspective, the report begins with the remarks of Professor Joseph White of the University of Michigan, a business educator and former corporate executive. He describes the building blocks that can lead to a quality revolution—a philosophy of continuous improvement, formal company-wide quality programs, and expanded training and education efforts.
- The culture of quality and the steps needed to start and implement the quality process are the subjects of papers from Hoechst Celanese, Eastman Kodak, and Management Science America.
- Executives from Corning Glass and L.L. Bean explain how superior external competition triggered a quality process that helped companies regain market share. Dramatic outcomes in the forms of cost savings and increased customer satisfaction are shown by Westinghouse's shrinkage of cycle time in plants and offices and by IBM's sharp reduction in defect rates in transistors, memory units, and microprocessors.
- Building quality into the management system and into the business strategy is illustrated in papers from Florida Power & Light, AT&T, and Hewlett-Packard.
- Examples of standards and measures of quality in improving administrative, technical and professional work are provided by executives from Metropolitan Life, the American Productivity Center, and the First National Bank of Chicago. A Ford manager discusses a prevention method

of statistical quality control and an experimental design technique for solving problems in the manufacturing process.

- Three speakers provided "case studies" in the nuts and bolts of delivering high quality in hospital care (Hospital Corporation of America), food and lodging (Marriott), and newspaper publishing (Gannett).
- Finally, the CEO of a key Xerox supplier (Nylomold) and a Xerox quality assurance manager share their experiences in a partnership that has lead to enhanced product quality for both parties.

Despite the accomplishments reported—and in many instances these are considerable—a common note sounded throughout the presentations is that it is still early days in the attempt to achieve total quality performance. There is much more to be learned and accomplished, and many more firms to be brought aboard before any real comfort can be taken. Yet speakers at this conference are confident that some of the signposts for the journey have been posted.

LAWRENCE SCHEIN

Part I
Setting the Agenda
for the Quality Revolution

Accelerating Quality Improvement

B. Joseph White

Associate Dean, Professor of Business Administration
The University of Michigan

Almost seven years ago, in the summer of 1981, Joseph Juran wrote an article in *Management Review* entitled "Product Quality—A Prescription for the West." It began with these words:

> The West is in serious trouble with respect to product quality. A major reason is the threat posed by the Japanese revolution in quality.

Juran acknowledged that Western quality had been improving since the early 1950s, but emphasized that the rate of improvement had not kept pace with the Japanese. He cited several industries—producers of color TVs, automobiles, and large-scale integrated circuits—in which Japanese manufacturers had begun to outperform their U.S. competitors in the mid-1970s. He then predicted flatly,

> During the 1980s, the situation will get worse, much worse.
> The magnitude of this threat has yet to be grasped by the West.

So where do we stand today, seven years later? Juran's observations were, of course, prophetic. Suffering from both a costly dollar and a perception of inferior quality, the U.S. auto, steel, machine tool, and consumer electronics industries, to cite familiar examples, have lost tremendous domestic market share as well as export opportunities.

The trade deficit is a reasonably good measure of the deterioration of the U.S. competitive position: Merchandise exports were $224 billion in 1986, the same as in 1980; imports over the same period rose nearly 50 percent, to $369 billion. In 1986, the U.S. trade deficit with Japan alone was $59 billion, compared with just $10 billion in 1980. And we experienced further deterioration in 1987, despite dollar depreciation.

So, just as Juran predicted back in 1981, things did get worse in the 1980s. The question is whether they are getting better now. I believe that we are turning the corner—we're late but we're underway and momentum is building. The next five years are going to be absolutely pivotal. I believe that the degree to which we improve our quality performance over this time period will determine

2

whether we achieve a strong competitive stature in the global economy or continue to suffer substantial losses. The quality performance of individual companies will make the difference between prosperity and weakness or death.

Several events have converged to make this the right time to shift from an evolutionary to an aggressive, revolutionary approach to quality improvement.

First, the weakened dollar permits many U.S. companies to be both price competitive and profitable domestically and internationally for the first time in years. Second, in the aftermath of the October 1987 stock market crash and the resulting decline in mergers and acquisitions, it is time to devote attention to the basics of operating our companies effectively. There have been many distractions in board rooms and executive offices in recent years. Quality improvement requires an intense focus on operations and a long view of performance.

Third, I find less defensiveness today on the part of managers about the reality of and reasons for quality problems. Fourth, and most important, I find a growing belief and gut-level conviction in senior managers that quality improvement really is the key to competitive success—to customer satisfaction, market share, productivity, cost reduction, and profit.

Unfortunately, the dedication we developed to quality improvement during the 1980s is checkered. Some companies made serious efforts to improve quality and are today reaping the benefits: in manufacturing, Ford, Maytag, and DEC; in services, Federal Express, American Airlines, and Disney are examples. The bottom line, however, is that many companies are not yet fully focused on quality and we are not yet leapfrogging the fast-moving competition.

The American Quality Revolution

What is required for us to achieve the American quality revolution in the next five years and beyond? How can we build on the momentum and accelerate the improvement already underway in many companies and involve the many more that are further behind? There are three essentials. The first requires U.S. managements to adopt an operating philosophy of continuous improvement in meeting customer needs and to support the rapid development of attitudes, policies, and management processes conducive to that philosophy. The second is to initiate many more formal programs of quality improvement. These should be customer focused, company wide, and heavy on employee involvement. The third is to reform our education and training programs so that they provide our people with the necessary knowledge and skills.

Continuous Improvement

"Continuous improvement" is the most powerful concept for guiding operating management that I have encountered. If we do not soon develop a whole generation of managers who understand and are dedicated to the pursuit of continuous improvement in meeting customer needs, I believe the current wave of interest in quality will pass and the performance gains we are achieving will not be sustained.

Continuous improvement requires a systematic process of planning and doing work, evaluating the results, locking in the current level of performance from which to improve further, and modifying the way work is done in the next cycle in line with what was learned from evaluating the results of the first. This systematic process must be tightly linked to a continuous assessment of customer needs. It depends on a constant stream of ideas and innovations about how to improve products and services from the customer's viewpoint and how to do things better. Continuous improvement requires a high degree of involvement and a sense of personal responsibility on the part of people doing the work. And, it requires continuous investment in all of the work-producing elements that determine results: processes, systems, equipment, and people.

Management's focus in a continuous improvement company is on the quality of products and services, and on the work system that produces them. I recognize that today there is an infatuation with strong individual leaders—the cult of the CEO—and with bold strategic moves as the real determinants of business success. My view is that strong CEOs are important, as is good strategy. But the companies with staying power are those with strong teams of operating managers who understand their business and are dedicated to the principles of continuous improvement in serving customer needs.

Four such principles are of central importance. First, focus on the customer. The purpose of all work and of all improvement efforts is to better serve customers. So, we must always know how well we are performing in the eyes of the customer. This means measurement and feedback. And it means constant innovation in products, services, and methods of operation. Of course, the most important customers are those who buy the company's product or services, but "customer" is also the next unit in the flow of work. Internal customers must be served for external customers to be served well.

Second, understand what determines performance and improve it. This means understanding flows and eliminating bottlenecks; focusing intensely on the design and control processes—both physical and managerial—that govern outcomes; and working closely with suppliers to improve their quality.

Third, involve all the employees in the improvement process. People are the source of ideas for improvement, and their cooperation is essential for implementation. We rely on the cooperation of our people to do things right and better. So, we have to reach out and involve them. Finally, for an organization to improve in the eyes of the customer, every phase of operations that touches the customer must improve. In light of our broad definition of customer, this means everyone must be involved.

Fourth, improvement can be seen as a "generic" process. A powerful and simple way to think about the improvement process is the repetitive Deming cycle of "plan-do-check-act" portrayed in a ratcheted, stair-step diagram, with each step representing a new level of standardization in the work process.

I encourage you to examine every major policy, practice, process, and system used to manage your operation and ask: "Does this contribute to continuous improvement?" The honest answer is often "No." For example: Plans and budgets are often seen as best-expected performance versus minimum-expected performance (i.e., as ceilings on performance versus floors from which to build improvement). We are also much better at building annual financial plans than at developing annual plans for operational improvement.

Measurement of effectiveness in manufacturing operations remains too rooted in cost-accounting methods that put direct labor under a microscope, while better measures of quality and efficiency, like cycle time, delivery performance, and support costs, often get inadequate attention. And, major processes and systems, like planning, product development, customer feedback, and performance reviews, are often not rigorously evaluated and upgraded after each major cycle. They are reused "as is" or, worse, simply scrapped and done differently next time.

Moreover, employees are sometimes expected to perform without a thorough understanding of the job and how to do it in the best possible way. People are moved and their assignments changed without regard to the impact on work improvement. I once worked with a fellow who said the answer to three simple questions should be "yes" before a person is moved. These are,

- Has the person learned the job?
- Has the person done the job?
- Has the person made substantial improvements in the way the job is done?

A lot of pay and job classification systems, especially those affecting hourly or salaried nonexempt people, create the impression among employees that they are paid only to do their jobs. Improving (that is, learning new skills, developing new capabilities, finding ways to do the work in a better way) is seen as extra and, when done, meriting extra pay. We must foster the understanding that improvement is part of everybody's job, every day.

Company-Wide Quality Programs

A quality revolution also requires the initiation of many more formal programs of quality improvement. Most companies today face the need for major transformation and a substantial ratcheting up of performance levels to meet new standards of competition. The questions facing management are: How do we launch the change process, mobilize the troops, set goals, and measure and recognize progress?

I believe that quality is by far the best program focus. Even companies faced with the need for substantial cost reductions are well advised to pursue them in the context of a quality-improvement program. Quality is a goal people rally around, unlike other operational goals, like cost reduction or productivity improvement. Quality opens people up to change, because the change is for a good reason. It connects them with the customer and taps the motive of pride in their work.

Education and Training

A quality revolution also depends upon major reforms in education and training. Education and training can be used either to maintain the status quo or as forces for change. We need the latter in our pursuit of quality improvement. This was clearly the case in Japan's "quality miracle," and it has been the experience of many successful U.S. companies. To succeed in this area, education and training must become a way of life. Five percent of every employee's time devoted to formal learning is a reasonable expectation and a big stretch from most companies' current practice. In addition, every employee must be included, and there should be a comprehensive curriculum, beginning with quality concepts and moving through the specific skills required to measure quality, identify problems, and devise and implement solutions. A full quality curriculum should be tailored for each major group of employees, since needs will vary according to function and level. And there should be a highly respected teaching staff.

Except for a small number of U.S. companies that have really effective quality-improvement programs and training to support them, training in U.S. companies is at present terribly deficient. The focus is more often on "how to do your job" than on "how to improve your operation." Or, the focus is on major topics like company strategy or overall direction, which are interesting, even important, but in which the individual has little direct involvement.

Managing Business School Curricula

University education also requires reform to support business' need for quality improvement. After returning to the business school world recently after seven years in industry, it is clear to me that quality and continuous improvement are critical missing elements in the core curriculum. Quality and continuous improvement should infuse the core curriculum. They are integrating concepts that can bring focus, purpose, and meaning to what are now loosely connected subjects, especially the cluster associated with managing operations, like strategy implementation, planning and control, managerial accounting, production and operations management, information systems, organizational behavior, and human resources management.

The opportunity lost by not putting quality and continuous improvement at the heart of the business school curriculum is great. The leading business schools attract young people of outstanding ability and leadership potential. Overall, U.S. business schools graduate 70,000 new MBAs per year. And a quarter of all undergraduate degrees granted annually are business majors. This means that we have direct access to hundreds of young people per year who can participate in and soon lead the American quality revolution, if only we prepare them properly.

More broadly, similar problems and opportunities exist in other areas of our educational system. For example, we produce many engineering specialists—industrial, mechanical, electrical, chemical, aeronautical, etc. But we may not be providing them with a framework, a body of concepts and an adequate understanding of quality and continuous improvement. Those essentials would enable them to make the greatest contributions to the competitive performance of their companies, whatever their engineering speciality. I have also found that industry compounds the problem by perpetuating narrow specialization and pegging those engineers most closely associated with quality, especially in operations, near the bottom of the technical pecking order.

Finally, I would like to point out that on a more fundamental level there is also a need for educational reform. A company's, or a nation's, ability to compete hinges on the capability, the knowledge, and the skills of its people. Unfortunately, the U.S. literacy rate is currently ranked 49th out of the 158 member countries of the United Nations. Twenty-seven million adult Americans (20 percent of the total) are functionally illiterate, and many more read on only the most minimal level. In addition, our high school dropout rate is a tragedy and disgrace.

We all know what is required for a workforce to contribute to quality: the ability and skills to read, to analyze and gather data to solve problems, to work in groups, and to develop as well as follow instructions. As a practical matter for individual companies, the current ability level of our adult workforce makes very tough-minded selection, or a commitment to a lot of remedial education, mandatory.

Part II
Starting Up Quality:
Basic Values and First Steps

Introducing the Quality Program in a Corporate Merger

Arthur B. Nichols, III
Director, Quality Management
Hoechst Celanese Corporation

In November 1986, we agreed to sell Celanese corporation to Hoechst A.G. of West Germany. Nothing has been the same since. Aside from combining two unpronounceable names into one impossible mouthful, it was—and is—a good deal for all parties. Consider the following:

(1) Celanese gave Hoechst a platform for expansion in North American markets as well as a base for serving world markets. With the acquisition, North America now represents almost a quarter of Hoechst's worldwide sales.

(2) Celanese has built strong marketing organizations for introducing new Hoechst products into the United States.

(3) The combination of Hoechst and Celanese polymer capabilities resulted in a company with the broadest range of materials for engineering plastics markets of any in the world.

(4) Compared to Celanese, at $3 billion in sales the new company is big—34,000 employees, $20 billion in sales, over a billion in annual R&D expenditures (second in the world).

With significant help from a strong marketplace, Hoechst Celanese achieved record earnings for 1987. The strength is across the board; all units have set profit records of their own.

But the real test of whether this merger will succeed lies in the ability of management to focus attention on the future. Can we establish and then communicate to every employee a clear vision of the kind of company we want to be and the goals we want to achieve? Some companies express this vision in a mission statement or a credo. In Hoechst Celanese we put it under the heading of values: the things we care about, the culture we want to establish, what we want to become.

What does this have to do with quality? Quality, itself, is a cultural value. At Celanese, quality was a total mind-set translated into action by means of processes we developed and applied to make the whole company run more smoothly and efficiently. We saw quality as a way of doing business, conducting relationships, dealing with customers, and practicing management.

In Hoechst Celanese, we have now set out, under the banner of quality, to define an explicit set of values for the new organization. We are using quality processes to bring together the best that both partners have to offer, but it is not going to be easy. On the plus side, there are many areas of commonality. Both the "Guiding Principles" of Hoechst A.G. and the "Goals and Values" of Celanese place special value on relationships with customers. Hoechst "sets its sights on a partnership. . . ." Celanese was "dedicated to understanding and meeting customer requirements."

Both companies believe in high performance standards. Hoechst "expects high standards...in every facet of its activities," and Celanese's goal is to be the "recognized quality leader" and achieve zero defects. Concern for people was likewise apparent in both cultural statements. At Hoechst, "the human being is the center of attention," and at Celanese, "respect for individuals and the contributions each can make" is a key value. But a culture is determined by what you do, not by what you say. And when looking at the practices of the two organizations, some real differences become apparent.

For example, with respect to employment continuity, a Hoechst goal is to provide jobs for more and more people, increasing employment to benefit society. Meanwhile, the name of the game at Celanese was to drive the headcount relentlessly down. Hoechst takes a long-term view of the business, with performance measures in sales growth and market share. At Celanese, managers were rewarded for maximizing short-term profits and cash flow, with the overall objective of increasing value to shareholders.

Organizationally, Hoechst employs a rather complex matrix management structure, which includes strong functional responsibility and authority at the top. Celanese was relatively streamlined and decentralized and had stretched line authority so far that function management was virtually nonexistent either at corporate or divisional headquarters. As a corollary to Hoechst's organization philosophy, multiple influences are brought to bear in decision making. A great many decisions are made at corporate HQ by senior managers who have the support of a large and powerful staff. Meanwhile, at Celanese, we had reduced corporate staff by 65 percent in the 1980s, and division managers were basically left to run their own shows as long as they lived up to their bottom-line commitments.

More fundamentally, Hoechst is a technology-driven company while Celanese was market driven. The Hoechst culture is described as "high chem," ours was more "high touch." Hoechst's mission is to develop and bring to market new products, based on its technology, that will benefit the world. Celanese, on the other hand, was a market opportunist. We succeeded mainly through our ability to spot new demand trends and develop, or if necessary, license the technology needed to get to the market fast. We were seldom first but almost always a close second. In R&D terms, Hoechst is R, Celanese was D.

Finally, although the quality programs of Hoechst and the former Celanese contained many of the same elements, our quality philosophies were quite different. In Hoechst, with some exceptions, quality was not viewed as a cultural issue requiring top management leadership and participation, while this had become an accepted and essential fact at Celanese. Hoechst had good, traditional product-oriented quality programs operated by Quality Control and Quality Assurance staff. At Celanese, we had these programs, but we also had, I concede with varying degrees of success, tried to extend quality beyond manufacturing plants into all areas of the business.

Looking ahead, our management task is to harmonize the cultures of the two merging organizations, build on their shared values, recognize and deal openly with their differences, while always integrating and evolving towards a culture that is uniquely our own.

The parent company in Frankfurt has given us the freedom to set goals and values based on what works best in the environment of our markets and business culture, and we have made a beginning. We have gathered ideas and suggestions from people at all levels of the organization as to the kind of place they would like this company to be and what goals they want to achieve.

Our values encompass performance goals and the way of achieving them through people and process (see Box). Far from perfect, and needing clarification and interpretation, these values are less important than the process by which they were developed—an open and participative method that has built a sense of ownership of these ethics, and that has demonstrated the values in practice.

Mergers fail for lots of reasons, but high on the list is failure of the partners to reach early, explicit agreement on a set of values to guide the new organization. As a result, actions and decisions can fall all over the lot, influenced by expediency, or worse, by politics, and can provide no consistent pattern, no clear message for people to follow—at the very time when clear, consistent leadership is most needed. As we see it, clarification of principles must come first, because decisions are driven, whether we realize it or not, by values. This is more critical than in a merger situation, where the decisions are big ones, and where your first chance is your best, or maybe only chance.

In deciding, for example, whom to appoint to key management positions in the new company, we are looking for people who practice values of participation, teamwork, and open communication and the performance appraisal system will reward these practices. In making decisions on organization structure—levels, span of control, numbers and types of staff groups, etc., we are trying to demonstrate trust and respect for individuals, and to encourage innovation and decision making at the lowest practical levels.

The new Hoechst Celanese values also establish the foundation for deciding compensation philosophy and practice. They clearly point towards compensation at the high end of industry scales to attract and retain people "consistently superior to competition." They require us to reward risk takers and not punish the inevitable failures and to provide recognition for quality achievement—not just a pat on the back, but financial recognition. Further, if we expect everyone to make a "commitment to continual improvement," then everyone should have the opportunity to share in the fruits of the improvement they help to bring about.

11

Hoechst Celanese Values

Performance

Preferred supplier, dedicated to understanding and meeting customer expectations;

Firm commitment to safety, employee health, and protection of the environment;

Responsible corporate citizen;

Earnings to support long-term growth;

Consistently superior to competition;

Commitment to continual improvement.

People

Respect for individuals and appreciation for contributions each can make;

Diversity accepted and valued;

Concern and fair treatment for individuals in managing business change;

Equal opportunity for each employee to achieve his or her potential;

Employee pride and enthusiasm;

Informed employees through open communication.

Processes

Openness and trust in all relationships;

Innovation, creativity, and risk taking encouraged;

Teamwork throughout the organization;

Participative goal setting, measurement, and feedback;

Decision making at the lowest practical level;

Actions consistent with clearly understood mission and long-term goals;

Recognition for quality achievements;

Resources committed to ongoing training and development.

The new Hoechst Celanese values stress the long-term picture: earnings to support long-term growth, decisions and actions consistent with long-term goals, and long-term commitment of resources to research and to employee training and development. To implement these values it is necessary to have organizational continuity, policies that encourage stronger contracts between people and their company, and the financial strength to support long-term commitments through low points in the business cycle.

We realized that putting the values on paper was just a beginning. The next step was to convene a two-day, off-site meeting of 130 top managers, at which we introduced and committed ourselves to act on these values. This meeting has set in motion a process of communication, interpretation, and action that will cascade down through the company over the next 6 to 12 months.

The rest of what we are doing to bring quality to Hoechst Celanese, while important, is pretty standard—a steering committee to provide overall quality leadership, a strong support organization headed by a corporate vice president of Quality and Communication, quality management teams at all divisions and sites, and functional quality councils. In the fall we will conduct an employee survey to check understanding of the new values, see how the merger is going, and establish benchmarks for measuring future progress.

Quality takes a beating in a merger—even in a friendly merger like ours—because of the inevitable anxiety that it causes people in the organization. Understandably worried about themselves, their horizons shrink, and they may no longer associate their future with that of the company. The practice of quality can be the force to help an organization and its people survive the trauma of merger. Quality is a universally accepted value. It can be the rallying point to start moving forward, the high ground from which people can begin to see the future.

It is critical to get values straight and to start practicing them even if we, as managers, are frantically busy, confronted with urgent decisions about the business and the merger, and concerned about our own jobs. We need to involve as many people as possible in the process because it will help to fix the new company's identity in the eyes of its people. And having values in place will help managers to provide clearer, more consistent leadership at a make-or-break time in the life of the new company.

LIBRARY ST. MARY'S COLLEGE

Total Organization Commitment: A Quality Ethic at Kodak

Ralph J. Rosati
Director, Corporate Quality
Eastman Kodak Company

When George Eastman founded Kodak in 1880, he pledged himself to produce "good goods" and believed strongly in this idea. For example, in the early years of photographic glass plates, photographers and dealers began to complain that the Eastman dry plates had lost their sensitivity. With thousands of dollars of plates in dealer stock, Eastman did something almost unheard of in those days. He recalled the whole lot and promised to replace all plates that didn't measure up to specifications. But try as he might to make a fresh emulsion, he could not produce a good one. The factory was closed. Weeks passed, and 469 successive experiments failed.

Finally, Eastman traced the problem to his gelatin supplier. The cows from which the gelatin came had fed on wild mustard seeds. Metabolized traces of the mustard in the gelatin were fogging the photographic emulsions. A new batch of uncontaminated gelatin finally solved the problem. The calamity nearly bankrupted Eastman's young company. But, he said, "What we have left is more important: our reputation." This episode is more than just an interesting historical aside. It illustrates the "quality ethic" in action: It is the courage to do the right thing for the customers.

In recent years, a series of events outside Kodak sent shock waves throughout our organization:

- The silver crisis brought unprecedented cost increases for basic materials.
- The overvalued dollar gave foreign companies an immediate and unearned price advantage.
- Many of our traditional markets came under increasing competitive pressure from manufacturers who came on the scene with products that competed very well with our own—in some cases, at more attractive prices.

The result? In the bull market of the early 1980s, Kodak was being described by many analysts as a company that had lost its direction. The facts were almost as bad—the financial results included flat sales and a 51 percent drop in earnings in 1983. Yet just four years later, *Fortune* magazine would include Kodak among seven companies in a special feature showing how "restructuring can make the U.S. competitive again." And *Barron's* described Kodak's performance as "a classic turnaround story."

That comeback was the direct result of a total organizational commitment to the "quality ethic"—the courage to do the right thing and to meet or exceed our customers' expectations. That meant we had to focus on four elements.

Sweeping Organizational Change

Kodak recognized that in order to identify and rapidly respond to customer needs, its organization structure needed overhauling. Kodak had been organized along functional lines. These divisions—such as manufacturing, marketing, and product development— often tended to insulate functional managers from the customers they ultimately served. Moreover, Kodak had been a two-unit company— photography and chemicals. Today, in contrast, Kodak operates 22 individual business units organized on a line-of-business basis within five major business groups: Photographic Products, Commercial and Information Systems, Diversified Technologies, Eastman Chemicals Division (see Box), and Life Sciences. Each business unit within the umbrella group functions as a "company within a company," and each is run by managers with worldwide, bottom-line responsibility for their products.

Management Participation

Our management had to personally take part in the quality ethic commitment. Kodak's renewed emphasis on improving quality began in 1983-1984, with the formulation of a corporate quality policy statement, part of which reads: "The Eastman Kodak Company is committed to be the world leader in the quality of its products and services. We will judge this quality by how well we anticipate and satisfy customer needs."

Quality of Material Aids Quality of Life

Our knowledge of customer needs and expectations and of how we can meet them is critical to providing the best possible materials. For example, the Eastman Chemicals Division has been the sole supplier of hollow-fiber membranes, which are made from Eastman cellulose acetate for use in artificial kidneys. Cellulose acetate is the material of choice for this application because it is inert and causes no allergic reaction. Made through an extrusion process, more than 13,000 hollow fibers the size of human hair are used in each kidney filter and these must be compatible with blood/body functions.

The company in Miami, Florida, that buys the membranes is the only U.S. manufacturer of these devices. Through constant improvement, the cellulose acetate has contributed significantly to blood dialysis through shorter treatment times, biocompatibility of materials, and manufacturing processes that leave no residual chemicals.

We needed not only a management commitment to quality but also a way of translating that commitment into action and accountability. To accomplish this, Kodak uses a number of programs including:

- Annual worldwide quality conferences to recognize quality-improvement efforts and to share methodology;
- Visits by top management to sites where quality improvement efforts are encouraged and improvement is monitored;
- Training in basic statistical techniques at all levels.

But one of the most effective mechanisms is personal quality-improvement projects. It's human nature to make more progress on a problem if it's "legitimized" by being made a project. A project can more effectively compete for attention, personnel, facilities, and services.

Everyone in management at Kodak, including our Office of the Chief Executive, is working on specific, clearly defined personal quality-improvement projects. Here are a couple of examples:

- Frank Strong is Group Vice President and General Manager of our Diversified Technologies Group. The goals of his personal quality project are to continue to focus on customer satisfaction. This includes listening more attentively to the customer; finding better ways to quantify and measure customer satisfaction; and improving the ways in which we quantify the linkages among customer requirements, product development, productivity, and product quality.
- Bill Prezzano is Group Vice President and General Manager of our Photographic Products Division. The major elements of his personal quality project are to cut the traditional product realization cycle time in half within two years and to foster a process for technology planning that is consistent with corporate business strategies.

Diverse as these two examples are, I think you can see that they share certain common characteristics. Each will be perceived as important and critical to the organization's success. Each relates to significant business objectives and can be measured in terms of its quality-improvement objectives.

Ongoing Improvement

The "quality ethic" requires continued quality improvement, not reaching a certain quality level and staying there. That's especially true when quality-improvement methods are applied to the service or white-collar side of a business or to special applications. Unfortunately, these areas are perceived as more difficult to measure and improve. But, the task is easier when quality is defined as "the degree to which you meet or exceed your customers' expectations." We teach our service people to know who their customers are, their expectations, and where they stand on meeting those expectations.

Managers must support those people who make courageous decisions for their customers. All of us in business would acknowledge that any bad product that escapes to the marketplace can have a sweeping negative impact on the whole company, especially if the company has a single brand name, as Kodak does. The reputation we work so hard to build can be quickly lost. But what if improving quality costs money or means stopping production? That was the decision faced recently by one of our production managers, who stopped an emulsion coating machine to bring the process to a higher standard. Shutting down one of these gigantic machines is not a casual act. They run 24 hours a day, 365 days a year. So this manager's decision meant significant production losses.

My point is not that the manager did the right thing—clearly he did. But let's face it, stopping production takes courage. Yet, the "quality ethic" requires having the courage to do what is right to meet customers' expectations, even when it is difficult or costly, and that means creating an environment which reinforces and rewards courageous people at all levels.

I don't want to give the impression that our quality improvement progress has been a smooth, steadily rising curve. It hasn't. Certainly there have been obstacles and setbacks, so our progress has been stair-step. However, quality-management principles are beginning to be applied to all facets of our business. And, led by top management, more and more employees are becoming involved. Our overall goal is to create an environment in which customer-oriented decision making and total quality commitment permeate all levels of the corporate culture. But if there is a single essential element, I believe it is getting and keeping top management involved.

Quality Improvement at MSA

Edward J. Kane
Vice President, Quality
Management Science America, Inc.

Five points are critical to the success of any quality-improvement effort. First, gain commitment at all levels; second, organize the effort; third, educate the people; fourth, establish improvement priorities; and fifth, manage the work.

Gaining Commitment

Commitment is important at all levels, but what does it really mean? Too often people believe that there's commitment at the top because the CEO signed a quality policy letter. Obviously, it's more than that.

The commitment of the senior executive or the CEO is absolutely essential, but not sufficient. One of the jobs of the top executive is to make sure that the line executives are involved. In my opinion, maintaining a quality improvement effort means it must fall within the responsibilities of line management. The line organization must accept responsibility for continuous quality improvement and weave it into the fabric of the business. If not, it will remain a "program" forever. The commitment to quality also means a willingness to communicate and give direction and review. If a review process is not put in place at the beginning, the effort will stall.

How do you really know when you have commitment? I think the test is whether the CEO is willing to change his own behavior, if that's required. If his thinking is exclusively short-term, or if his style is not participative enough, the change must start with him. A commitment to continuous improvement changes one's mind set from simply conforming to requirements to moving beyond conformance. We must move from problem solving to prevention and, finally, to improving everything for the sake of effectiveness and efficiency.

Another aspect of commitment from the CEO involves tying quality in with the compensation and bonus plan. That is one sign of whether the CEO is committed or is simply giving lip service to quality efforts.

Commitment from middle management is also critical because managers are the implements of change in a company. But, problems are most likely in this area. Convincing middle management to change is tough because they've been successful. They've been promoted because of how well they've acted as crises managers in the past. Now suddenly someone is telling them to change their approach and be more participative in style. Not surprisingly, there's resistance.

To overcome this reluctance, direction and communication about quality improvement must be clear. There must be a hierarchy of measurements utilized at the task level (defect oriented) and at the top (primarily financially oriented). A regular review structure is essential for continuing focus.

Organizing the Effort

The central quality staff is best made up of people who are knowledgeable about functions of the company or business units. We should not be overly concerned with having people who understand quality; that can be learned. What people can't acquire quickly and easily is experience and credibility in the company's business. The quality staff should also be small to emphasize that quality is a line management responsibility. At Management Science America (MSA) the central staff is small, but there is a quality coordinator for each vice president of a major area (e.g., development, sales, administration, and personnel). The central quality staff invests a lot of time and effort in educating those people so that they will become the quality drivers in their organizations.

To coordinate the efforts, I suggest that each executive—for example, the vice president of development—appoint a quality council consisting of that executive and his direct reports. The group functions as a committee to review the approach being taken on quality issues, the progress made, and the results.

Educating the People

Teaching the values of continuous quality imporovement involves making people aware of the basic concepts as well as presenting the tools and techniques necessary. But education without action has no value. So education in any detailed form should only be undertaken before a major improvement effort gets underway. At MSA, my major effort in education will be through the process-improvement teams and the quality council. We use kickoff and update meetings for information purposes. The real education sessions last two to three days. There we present quality concepts for the people who are going into the process-improvement teams and tools and techniques for the quality professionals. A separate, outside educational effort is not necessary. At MSA we worked with the existing education organization and I believe that's best.

Prioritizing the Improvement

Prioritizing the improvement involves identifying critical success factors, problems, and opportunities. If there are existing problems, you must solve them first. It's also important to look at opportunities and at what is central to the mission of the organization. What are the important cost drivers or areas of competitive advantage on which you can concentrate and improve? It is most important to tap the creativity of the line people. They are the guts of the organization, best able to take charge, and the ones who can decide what to focus on in the quality improvement effort.

Continuous quality improvement should be tied to the strategic plan and the planning system. Too often companies have a separate quality plan. That's usually a mistake. Quality specific objectives must be worked into the existing planning structure, because later a transition will be difficult.

Managing the Work

Managing the work is really the essence of the quality effort, the culmination of the first four phases I discussed. How do real improvements happen? There are four critical ingredients for success. First, each person must have a sense of ownership of the work activity he/she manages. Often today either nobody owns it, or everybody owns it. Second, adopt a participative style. In my opinion, you can't be successful without it because continuous quality improvement is based on tapping the creativity of the people who understand the work best, who in turn are those closest to it. Third, measure your efforts. If you can't measure the work, you can't manage it. But not all measurement is or needs to be objective—if it's the customer's perception, it's reality. Fourth, assure yourself of quality products from vendors. You can't produce defect-free products or services if your input is defective.

In summary, every company must develop its own approach based on its culture, organization, and shared values. I believe, however, that the principles apply everywhere. Continuous quality improvement requires management leadership, line responsibility, focused education, participative decision making, and a disciplined approach to managing the work. With it comes improved effectiveness, efficiency, and competitive advantage.

Part III

Powerful Outcomes:
Market Share, Cycle Time, and
Defect Rates

Quality and Market Share

Richard Dulude
Group President
Corning Glass Works

Corning is a high-technology company with products and services for consumer, industrial, health-care, and scientific markets around the world. We make more than 50,000 different products, with industrial products accounting for about half of our sales.

Corning is on the front lines of some of the world's most hotly contested battlefields and the competition is fierce. We received an early bombshell in our television glass business and it offers a dramatic example of the effect of quality on market share. We were the innovators in the manufacture of high-quality, precision-made TV picture tubes. In fact, during the 1930s, Corning supplied the first glass to Alan Dumont when he invented television in his garage in New Jersey. We pioneered the development and production of the all-glass display bulb, the sealing glass compositions that weld the bulb together, the glass delivery systems, and the forming and finishing processes.

We committed large amounts of capital to production during the 1940s and 1950s in time to catch the twin booms for black-and-white and color television. However, using the basic technology developed by Corning, the Japanese became major forces in this market and were beating us at our own game! In the 1970s, the U.S. market began to slow and imports of television sets and picture tubes cut into the sales of our major domestic customers. Although our quality remained consistently good, our competitors were getting better.

We went from first place to last. But we decided that Corning was in the television business to stay, and realized that our staying power would be directly related to the quality of our products and service. Only with top-quality products would our customers be able to compete with foreign manufacturers.

We started with manufacturing operations and consolidated our operations in our State College, Pennsylvania, plant. We felt that by closely analyzing our process we could significantly improve its stability, resulting in better performance. After a thorough application of statistical process control techniques and a commitment of millions of dollars over a three-year period, we achieved the following results:

- Product specifications were tightened by 40 percent;
- The stability of some operations improved by as much as 50 percent;

- Output escalated by more than 20 percent and by as much as 40 percent on occasion;
- The dimensional variability of our end product was reduced by 17 percent.

Let me be even more specific. A customer can reject a panel, the front of a picture tube, if it has a blister, a defect as small as twenty-thousandths of an inch. With the improved process, our defect rate went from about 10,000 parts per million to around 1,000 parts per million. That's total quality at work. But the story doesn't end there. Our commitment to total quality has gone a lot further. We're asking all our employees to become ultimately responsible for what they produce. If there's something wrong, we don't want them to let the machine run. We want them to stop it, even if it means stopping the entire production line. We're simply not going to make or ship products that don't meet our customers' requirements, if we can possibly help it. The amazing thing is that we can help it.

And that is the way total quality works. It's a story of market share in the most dramatic sense—not a question of gaining a point or two of market share—not a matter of expanding Corning's slice on the latest pie chart but the ultimate issue of survival. Demand for our products is growing so rapidly that we've just completed a 175,000 square foot addition to the television bulb plant with a new glass furnace and a new production line. And, we're hiring about 100 more people.

What's happened at State College is happening all through Corning. Total quality is becoming our operational philosophy as well as our day-to-day work method. For example, Ford Motor Company is one of our biggest customers for the ceramic substrate used in emission-control systems. One day Ford came to us with a message. They let us know that people on the other side of the Pacific were making the product more in keeping with Ford's requirements, because they were way ahead of Corning in statistical process control (SPC). Ford thought we should radically improve our use of SPC at the substrate plant or we could expect to see more and more of the business going to the competition.

It was another incoming bombshell that hit us in a totally unexpected place. We pioneered the development of the substrate, we opened up the market, and we're a solid number one. In fact, we feel downright possessive about this market. With much effort we mastered SPC at the plant, but it took three years and that surprised us. At that time, we didn't understand what a complicated elusive goal you chase when you go after SPC. In retrospect, the bombshell from Ford was right on target. It forced us to go after quality in our substrate business and it reinforced our company-wide commitment to quality.

Since we responded to Ford's requirements for total quality, we've made an incredible impact on market share. For starters, we saved our existing market share and in the process created a whole new generation of processes, materials, and product enhancements. We significantly increased our domestic market share for substrates—to the point of needing additional capacity. We just removed the "for sale" sign from a plant where we formerly made industrial flat glass. The plant had been closed for three years; it's now reopened and substrate manufacturing is scheduled to start up later in 1988.

We also took our show on the road and grabbed the lead in Europe. A new Corning-built manufacturing facility is up and running, and we have secured the lion's share of a dynamic and growing European market. We are now positioned to take the lead in the booming Pacific Basin and South American markets, which are expected to burst wide open in the next three to four years. And for our grand finale, we doubled market share in Japan.

Corning's experience is not unique. With the current emphasis on competition, and with the shift toward a global economy, no business can survive without a genuine commitment to quality. The people who will succeed in this worldwide arena are those that provide the quality goods and services that the customer wants. It's that simple, because quality makes the critical difference between having market share and handing it to your competitor. Even more important, it makes the difference between survival and extinction.

But that brings me to some disturbing news. Results from a Gallup Poll commissioned last fall by the American Society for Quality Control showed that, while awareness of the need for quality is growing, there's still a long way to go. Most of the poll's respondents don't understand, first, the magnitude of the issue. They don't understand that blame shouldn't be aimed at the workers. They grossly underestimate the importance of leadership. For example, most managers seem to think that the cost of poor quality isn't very much. Sixty-seven percent of the managers interviewed in the Gallup poll said the cost of quality is under 10 percent of annual sales. That's just wrong. Simply stated, the cost of poor quality—the cost of preventing and detecting and paying for errors—is somewhere between 20 and 30 percent of sales for the average company.

Companies that have concentrated on quality have been able to cut that figure in half. But recognizing the cost of poor quality is not enough. Real commitment—through education and top management—is essential. When we began the total quality journey at Corning, we started what we call the Quality Institute. It's a school for quality—and everybody has to go. In fact, I was in the first class with the chairman, the vice chairmen, and other top managers. So far, we've put 28,000 employees through the school, almost all of our worldwide employees. At the school, we mix up all levels of employees, because everybody has good ideas and is concerned about improving the company's quality record.

Overall, our commitment to training is enormous. We've built special classrooms, trained our own instructors, and translated our Quality Awareness training program into Spanish, Portuguese, German, French, and even into the Queen's English. We've established a goal of dedicating 5 percent of all time worked—that's 1.5 million worker hours a year—to quality training over the next three years. But it pays off. Training is so cost effective because it's preventive. It teaches not only how to solve problems but also how to prevent them before they occur. The goal of our training is ultimately to help teach our employees to discover how to do the best possible job so that the job only has to be done once.

Quality starts at the top. Quality demands an ongoing commitment from top management. It can't be just a put-on attitude, a slogan. If so, it will fail. It has to be at the heart of organizational philosophy. It's got to be a stated value, a part of the mission statement—and it has to be lived every day.

Those examples from our TV glass and ceramic substrate business are the best illustrations I can offer. Employees at every level responded to the challenges and participated as a team has never before. Now that managers and workers have experienced the results of true partnership, they are the ones who champion and treasure teamwork. The kind of quality we are talking about is the wave of the future. The world is shrinking and those of us who intend to be players in this new global economy had better understand that quality is the name of the game.

Value-Driven Business = Long-Term Success

Thomas C. Day
Vice President, Fulfillment Operations
L.L. Bean, Inc.

L.L. Bean invented the Maine hunting shoe in 1912, and out of the first 100 pairs sold, 90 came back and were replaced. The return rate has since improved, but we still honor L.L. Bean's original guarantee: "All of our products are guaranteed to give 100 percent satisfaction in every way. Return anything purchased from us anytime it proves otherwise." There are no time limits, no conditions. The underlying values that drive our business are known internally as L.L.'s golden rule: "Sell good merchandise at a reasonable profit and treat your customers like human beings, and they'll always come back for more." That rule forms the cornerstone of our mission statement.

There are also several corollaries in our corporate culture including: "We only sell what we ourselves use." Examples include such programs as outdoor experience for management, product testing trips, and an overall employee knowledge of products and services second to none in our industry. We've been able to combine this product testing with team-building exercises and the result is a real sense of shared value. When you spend six days in the rain on the Allagash River or climb several mountains with your co-workers, you get to know the people in your organization.

So far we've been successful with these basic values. The company grew steadily from its founding in 1912 through two World Wars and the Depression to reach about $3 million in sales by 1965. At that time, L.L. Bean was in his 90s and was slowing down. Leon Gorman, our current president, succeeded his grandfather and an uncle, both of whom died in 1967. He rejuvenated the product line, reaffirmed his grandfather's traditional values and way of doing business and started an aggressive marketing program. Our growth has been remarkable. We've gone from $3 million in sales in 1965 to $300 million in 1985. There have been no acquisitions or mergers, and in our 75 year history we have had only three presidents.

Our growth has not been entirely smooth, however, and we have been tempted to compromise our values. In 1982, for example, we had a pretty good year. The "preppy" look was at its height and we won a Coty Fashion Award for selling the very same products we'd been carrying for 40 years! Demand was up 31 percent from the year before, net sales were up 27 percent, and we had a 39 percent return on equity. In 1983, the Grinch showed up and had a sobering effect on a company that had had a 30 percent compound growth rate for 15 years. Demand still grew by 5 percent but income was down by 21 percent.

There were two schools of thought on how we should respond to this situation. Many of us in management wanted to focus on profitability through a productivity improvement program that sought to identify product offerings that would improve margins and appeal to a broader segment of the population. We considered charging for postage and handling, as most of our competitors do. Most charge $3 to $6 for postage; we consider it an operating expense. This year a $1 charge would add $7 million to our bottom line. We also considered limiting alterations, special orders, merchandise information, and other areas in which we spend a lot of money servicing our customers. In addition, we considered expanding into retailing, as have many of our competitors, including Talbots, Eddie Bauer, and Banana Republic.

While we were thinking of ways to maintain good profitability in a world of rising new-customer acquisition costs, tight margins, and increasing postal and shipping fees, Leon Gorman was focusing on long-term success for the business and its place in society. He looked at the business and saw a lack of product innovation, with a declining number of products among our top sellers. Our focus had been on low-cost, high-efficiency fulfillment service, which resulted in an internal process time that ranked 13th against 15 competitors. We could not accurately forecast nor maintain the high—88 percent to 90 percent—initial in-stock positions that Leon Gorman thought were essential for quality service. The remedy announced was a new quality policy: L.L. Bean would be "quantifiably" the best at what it does. We would offer the best products, provide the best service, and give the best functional value to the customer.

Over the next two years, we made major strides using that strategy. In the product area, we began a major reorganization and an expansion of the function to develop innovative products and to meet our customers' needs. We expanded our lab and field testing areas, and both currently play a critical role in screening products and evaluating how they stack up against the individual products of competitors. We've done extensive research into what our customers want and how to improve the value of what we offer them. We've also developed a product utility matrix to provide a comprehensive assessment of where we stand vis-a-vis products from a number of catalogers appealing to the same customer base. In other words, we can determine whether we're quantifiably the best.

On the service side of the business, there has been a major upgrading of computer support to provide for our inventory management function. Our internal cycle time was reduced from over seven days to about three days through major procedural changes. We started a nation-wide, toll-free telephone service in 1986 at an annual cost of over $8 million. We've continued free shipping, and we offer a flat $7 service charge for Federal Express. The customer service matrix has allowed us to measure our performance against our competitors' and to ensure that we are quantifiably the best at what we do.

Did we do all the right things? From the sales perspective, we seem to have recovered nicely, adding $50 million in new business in 1985, $65 million in 1986, and more than $100 million in 1987. We're also seeing a higher response rate to our mailings, increases in the average order value, and a strong growth in our customer list. We've seen dozens of magazine and newspaper articles praising our services and products in the last year or so. The article that has pleased us most is the October 1987 *Consumer Report* evaluation of mail order companies based on responses from 200,000 people. L.L. Bean ranked #1 in virtually every product category in which it was evaluated.

As customer satisfaction becomes more critical, greater importance must be placed on educating employees in the values and services that drive our business. We do 15 percent of our annual business in two weeks, and 25 percent of our annual business in four weeks. So temporary employees are clearly linked to our success. Last fall, we had 822 telephone operators just taking customer orders. Ninety percent of them had been hired since the first of September. Our values, which are clearly and consistently communicated to all employees, provide a strong sense of direction and allow the decision-making process to be pushed down in the organization. We believe that a value-driven business can lead to long-term success, as long as you stick to the business that you know.

Go With the Flow—Measuring Information Worker Quality

George C. Dorman
Vice President, Human Resources
Westinghouse Electric Corporation

Every summer, we are inundated by the Japanese. They flock to American businesses with tape recorders, cameras, and a thousand questions. A large number visit Westinghouse each year. Until recently, our Japanese visitors were mainly interested in touring our factories. Now their focus is changing—they want to know about the productivity and quality procedures in our offices. This is a very significant change that signals some good news for the United States. It is clear that the ability to leverage the knowledge and expertise of white-collar workers' activities is now a dominant factor in our ability to compete globally.

The key to cost competitiveness today is no longer the factory worker. It is the information worker, the so-called white-collar force. Our future success will depend on how well we can leverage this expertise and capability. Overall, the United States enjoys a leadership position in this crucial, high-cost area. We have the opportunity—right now—to build on this lead and to expand on our world market position.

In Westinghouse, information workers now represent two-thirds of our workforce. That's over 75 percent of our total payroll costs, and those proportions are increasing. Our largest occupational group is engineers, followed by clerical people, salespeople, and accountants. These information workers are also a major key to quality performance. Our studies show that nearly two-thirds of our costs-of-quality failures are due to white-collar issues—not factory problems.

At Westinghouse, our total quality effort is a cornerstone of corporate strategy. Eight years ago we founded the Westinghouse Corporate Quality Center, and today, with 220 employees, it may be the largest of its kind in the world. As you might expect, nearly two-thirds of the Center's activities are currently focused on white-collar performance, both in terms of productivity and quality. We're still making impressive gains in factory performance—with just-in-time practices and so on, but the most significant total quality improvements are coming from white-collar workers.

Two powerful improvement tools help us get our arms around the total quality process. One was initially developed for use in the factory as a way to reduce inventories dramatically. It involves cutting process cycle time by an average of 60 to 70 percent, with resultant cost reductions of 25 percent or more. This is no small achievement. Using this technique, Westinghouse operations have cut factory inventory levels by more than $700 million over the past three years. But that's only the beginning. We also discovered that cycle time is also a powerful lever for improving office operations. Its potential for improving white-collar processes is even more dramatic than in the factory.

Cost-Time Profiles

Our goal is to radically reduce cost and time by improving processes. One good way to analyze a process—whether it's a manufacturing activity in the plant or an order-entry system in the office—is to study its cost-time profile. Every process has a unique profile that illustrates the aggregation of costs over time.

In Chart 1, the shaded area represents investment in the business—its cash! In the factory, this takes the form of inventory that we can count—either raw materials, works-in-process, or finished-goods inventory. In the office, it's less tangible—it's knowledge, data, paper, and information— but it still represents cash spent on the business. The goal of process improvement is to shrink this profile. Obtaining the same result with significantly less cash investment is a powerful way to build value and gain competitive advantage. And by far the most effective improvement lever we have found is cycle time.

Quality and cycle-time reduction are directly related—as Chart 2 shows. When quality of product and performance improves, cycle time comes down—because you're eliminating rework and false starts, as well as reducing organizational

Chart 1

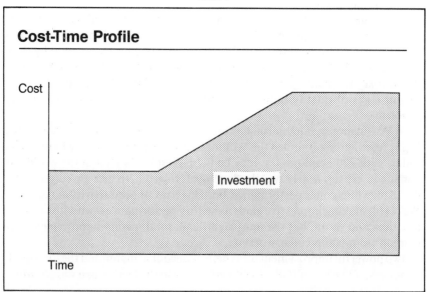

redundancy. Looking at it another way, working to reduce cycle time forces you to improve your quality performance. In either case, working on the existing process will eventually get you to the zero defects stage, with an associated minimum cycle time.

Every process has an associated cost-time profile, which is the "current" profile on Chart 3. Working on the time and quality elements, we can definitely shrink the profile, as indicated by the profile labeled "planned" on the same chart.

Chart 2

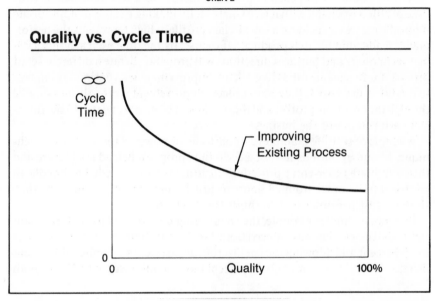

Chart 3

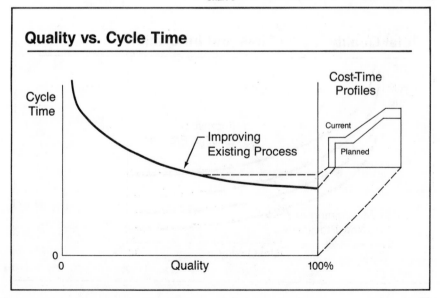

Clearly, the way to continue improving is to innovate. We need to introduce new and better ways to do the process job in every one of our activities: field, and factory, office and shop, line and staff. Each significant innovation achieves a leap to a new, improved curve (see Chart 4). That's how we continuously improve our potential for cycle-time reduction. Obviously, in each case we must also work to bring our quality performance up to 100 percent, in order to realize the full potential of the cycle-time savings.

As you would expect, each innovative process has a new and smaller cost-time profile associated with it (see Chart 5). By making a series of appropriate innovations, we can achieve a world-class profile, which represents the performance leadership for that product. Of course, by the time we reach this level, new technology and business directions will probably dictate a different set of process improvements for us to work on; improvement is a continuous imperative. Notice, in Chart 5, that every process improvement is directly measurable through the cost-time profile; and the profile can be directly related to the financial performance of the business.

A couple of real-life examples demonstrate the power of this cycle-time technique. In one of our businesses, a cycle-time program helped restructure and then automate order-entry procedures, cutting the time needed to handle an electrical parts order from 28 hours to just 10 minutes and at the same time slashing cost per order by two-thirds (see Chart 6).

In a more complex example, the engineering design cycle for nuclear plant fuel reload assemblies was reduced from 3 years to 18 months, lowering the costs by 25 percent and allowing the engineering department to handle a 40 percent increase in workload with only 10 percent more people (see Chart 7). For both

Chart 4

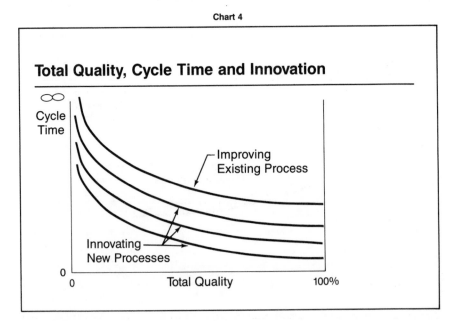

instances the technique was the same: first, streamline the process; then apply the technology to implement the new, improved process. You can't do it in reverse order. In both cases, these were important white-collar processes: one in marketing, the other in engineering.

Similarly, we use a proprietary, computerized technique called Organization Profile to examine information flow and work patterns in office operations.

Chart 5

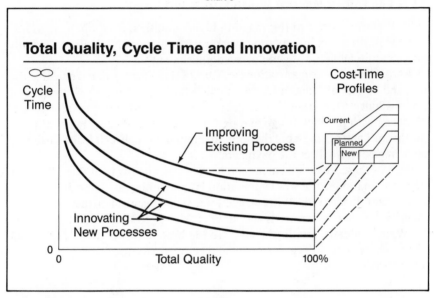

Chart 6

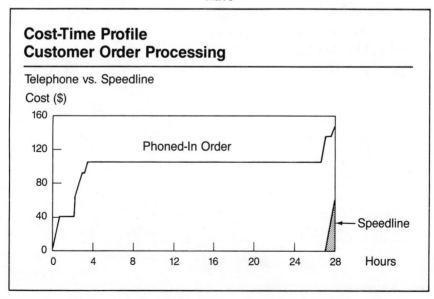

The analysis can point us to optimal organization structures, reporting links, spans of management control, and the like. It's a way to use our process know-how to structure the best organization for world-class office work. At one Westinghouse division, the Organization Profile analysis showed the division manager how to restructure his pre-manufacturing operations for dramatically better customer service, while reducing manpower level by 37 percent.

Process Improvement in Management

Now, how is change of this magnitude accomplished for a whole organization? How do we set information-worker performance and quality standards and measure and reward genuine accomplishment?

A typical business organization (see Chart 8) has general management at the top, and a series of functions, each of which has a specific area of interest and responsibility. Marketing is concerned about sales and customer service; engineering with product design and performance; manufacturing about making the stuff and getting it out the door, so shipping can deliver it to the customer, and finance can collect the payments.

Each of these functional areas can be very skillful at what it does. But that does not guarantee the whole operation is functioning at a world-class level to meet customer's needs. What we really want is an organization that can rapidly identify those customer needs and move efficiently to satisfy them (see Chart 9). What generally gets in the way are the boundaries between functional departments—the walls we seem to build between each area of special interest and expertise.

Chart 7

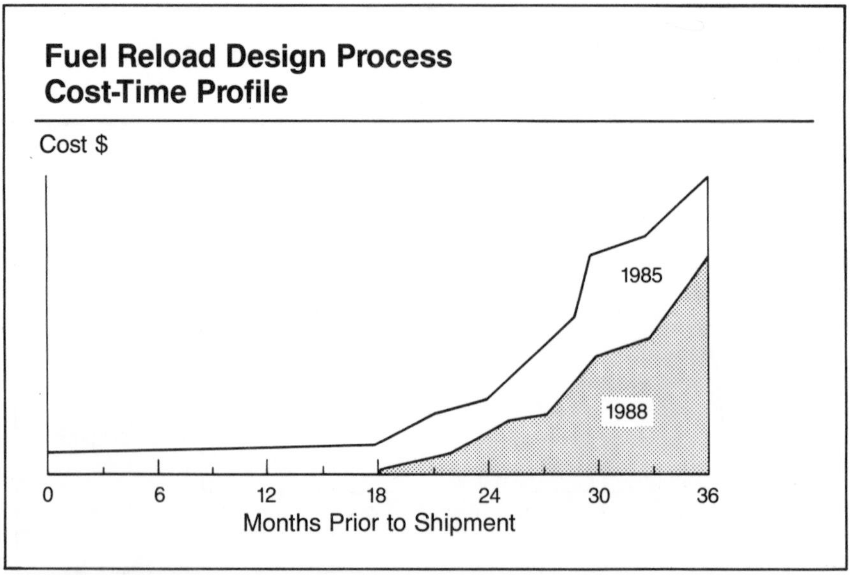

**Fuel Reload Design Process
Cost-Time Profile**

Cost $

1985

1988

0   6   12   18   24   30   36

Months Prior to Shipment

What doing business is really all about is performing a series of interlocked processes, starting with sales and going through order entry, resource planning, production, distribution, and payment collection. Not one of these basic business processes is performed within the walls of one single functional department. All of them are, almost by definition, multi-functional. Now what happens as we pursue a customer and then move to satisfy his need for performing these

Chart 8

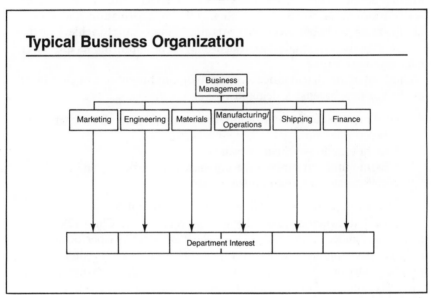

Chart 9

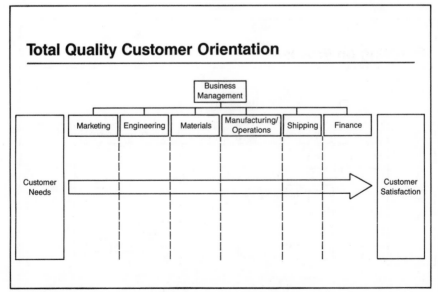

processes every day? Do we get a smoothly flowing integrated operation, with a minimum cost-time profile and 100 percent quality performance (see Chart 10)?

Probably not. Too often, we operate with a less than truly efficient process (see Chart 11) in which, for example, the customer's order often bounces back and forth between functions, before it finally moves on to the next step in the overall process. This inefficient back-and-forth effect is caused by the need to clarify information, correct errors, obtain missing information, and so on. In this operating mode, overall excellence is almost impossible to achieve, no matter how effective any single department may be at improving its quality and reducing its cycle time.

This kind of inefficient process is what balloons the entire cost-time profile for the business because it demands:

- Extra people and organization structure to manage all the interfaces between functions;
- Extra time to get them shipshape;
- Extra money to support the organizational expenses and quality problems such a system inherently spawns.

Total quality requires process innovation in this overall business process just as much as it does in individual, day-to-day processes (see Chart 12). We want to achieve a smoothly integrated flow, where every activity performs its part of the process to optimize total performance. That's how we can eliminate traditional interface problems between functions and slash the extra organizational costs they produce. The total quality process includes everything from inves-

Chart 10

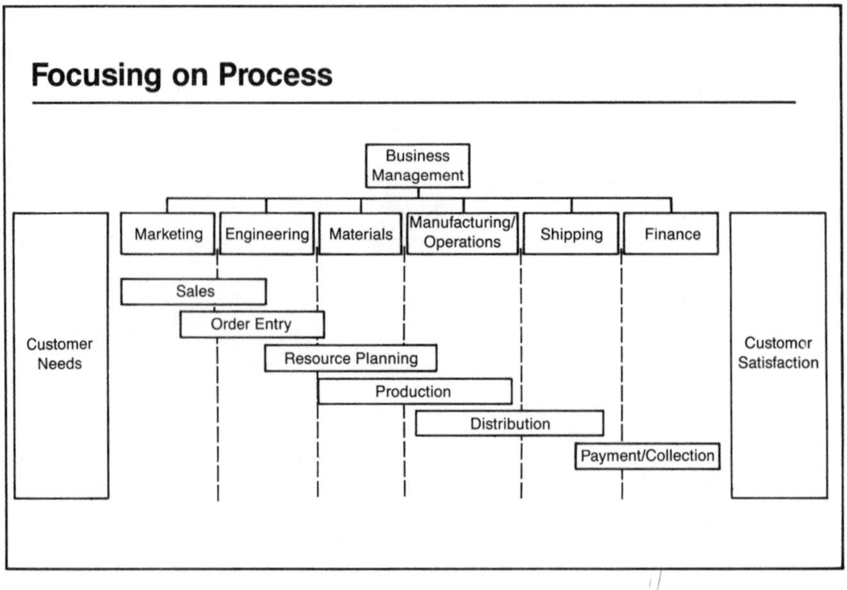

Focusing on Process

	Business Management		
Marketing	Engineering	Materials	Manufacturing/Operations	Shipping	Finance

Customer Needs

Sales

Order Entry

Resource Planning

Production

Distribution

Payment/Collection

Customer Satisfaction

tigating customer needs and establishing customer requirements, to establishing resource requirements, producing and delivering the product or service, and invoicing and collecting payment. The end result is customer satisfaction based on continuous and improving performance. Such excellence is readily measurable and rewardable.

Chart 11

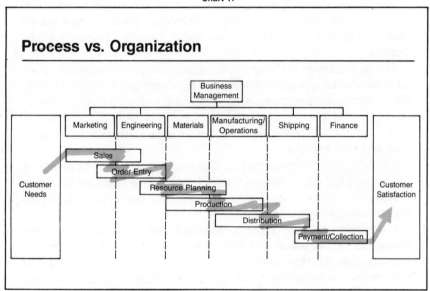

Chart 12

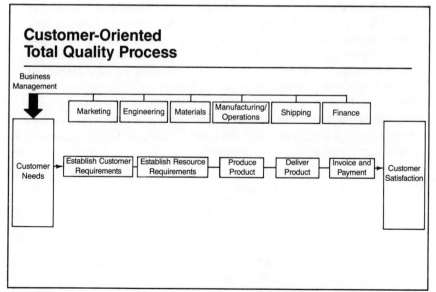

Our Assemblies Division faced a particularly difficult problem a couple of years ago. Total market volume for their electrical panelboard and switchboard products was declining. The emphasis in the construction business they serve was shifting from big projects to small, harder-to-serve jobs. It was a very tough marketplace, with a lot of aggressive competitors seeking to get orders from the very tough, savvy electrical contractors who buy and install panelboards and switchboards.

The product itself had over 2400 possible components, which could be assembled in a virtually limitless variety of configurations. As a result, order negotiation was complex and required a lot of up-front engineering, so the costs to us to quote a job were very high. Once an order was obtained, it typically required special shop work, which is expensive and time consuming.

What I'm describing is a classic dilemma for a mature business. Fine tuning was not going to turn things around. The need for dramatic action—innovative action—was very clear, and was recognized by division management as imperative.

From the toolbox we use to pursue total quality, this division chose to apply design for value, which is a complete and comprehensive systems approach to the product-development process. It calls for a full-time, multi-functional team—in this case including people from Engineering, Manufacturing, Marketing, Process Planning, and Information Systems. They were from a number of different division locations from the Midwest, the South, and Pennsylvania.

The team members were detached from their regular duties so they could devote full time to the project. In theory, the team focuses on a broad mission, so that its members quickly lose their functional bias—and are free to integrate their functional expertise to achieve an optimal solution. Our team's mission was to develop a totally integrated system for a new product line of panelboards and switchboards. They worked on the total business process—not only the product engineering design, but also the front-end marketing and customer requirements, through negotiation and order entry, manufacturing processes, installation, and service requirements.

In the course of the project, the team developed three particularly significant innovations: a powerful marketing strategy; a new, automated negotiation and order entry system; and a redesigned product line along with new manufacturing processes to effectively produce it. The result was a brand new panelboard/switchboard line with some new features. For instance, by carefully identifying customer requirements, the team members standardized on just eight configurations, which cover over 90 percent of the market's requirements. This approach dramatically simplifies everything—including procurement, parts stocking, manufacturing, and the product order process.

They developed a computerized negotiation and order system entry, part of it using an artificial intelligence program, which automatically selects the appropriate configuration for the customer's application. This approach reduces both front-end engineering time and expense, as well as quotation response time back to the potential customer—a real competitive advantage.

The team's redesign cut those 2400 product elements in half, improving not only manufacturability but also quality and reliability. The group also reduced the physical dimensions of the unit, a real benefit to the electrical contractor customer and another competitive advantage. They also revamped virtually the entire manufacturing procedure and made two especially outstanding innovations. Parallel processing of subassemblies, allowing them to come together in "just-in-time" fashion at final assembly, had a tremendous effect on reducing the cost-time profile for manufacturing. And, designing the product to use existing tooling on the world-class flexible manufacturing system already in place eliminated the need for costly retooling.

Normally, a complete product development of this type takes about 36 months. Our team did it in just 18 months using the design for value process—cutting the development cycle-time by 50 percent. Cycle-time from receipt of customer order to product delivery was cut in half. And, overall costs and inventory were both reduced 30 percent.

Quality in the Global Marketplace

Kaspar V. Cassani
Executive Vice President
International Business Machines Corporation

IBM has seen tremendous growth in the computer and information process-ing industry. Strong new competitors have emerged worldwide and they under-stand quality very well. About ten years ago, our customers began telling us that our products could be better. So we stepped up our efforts to respond to their concerns and established strict measurements to evaluate performance. We conducted extensive surveys of customer reactions and began to raise stan-dards on a continual basis. Significant improvements in product performance and reliability include:

- Million-bit memory chips: Since we introduced them two years ago, not a single one of our customers has been dissatisfied.
- The IBM 3090: Our most advanced computer uses as many as 132 chips, which are mounted on a ceramic carrier about 3½ inches square and interconnected through as many as 470,000 tiny holes. More than 3 million of these carriers have been shipped in the last seven years without a single failure at a customer's location.

Significant progress has also been made with joint efforts between IBM and the manufacturers and suppliers we work with, especially in the areas of tran-sistors, memories, and microprocessors. As these figures show, the improve-ment between 1980 and 1987 in acceptable defect rates is huge:

Acceptable Defect Rate
(per million)

	1980	1987
Transistors	2,800	55
Memory units	8,200	120
Microprocessors	4,800	180

Improved Manufacturing

But total quality means more than high reliability and low defect rates. It means upgrading the manufacturing process—how work is done. Three years ago, we found that eliminating individual defects yielded only marginal improvements. To make greater gains in productivity and efficiency, we needed to direct our attention toward manufacturing cycles, in particular their length.

Shorter manufacturing cycles (1) make us more responsive to our customers, (2) use smaller inventories, (3) require fewer buffers to protect against contingencies, (4) lead to lower costs, and (5) result in lower-priced products. Our "ProPrinter," for example, was developed in just 13 months. Under our former methods, development would have taken three or four years.

Furthermore, the drive for quality should not be confined to new products and technologies. Significant improvements can be made with existing products. Our Selectric typewriter, for example, was the best on the market for more than 20 years, but in the late 1970s we set out to make it even better. We improved the quality of the components and the manufacturing processes, leaving the typewriter design and its 25-year-old technology unchanged.

The results? Warranty repair rates dropped by about a third, and the savings in costs were passed on to the bottom line.

Quality Service

Even these extensive improvements do not suffice, however. Today, the emphasis must be on solving customer problems and delivering superior service. Reliable, well-manufactured products themselves cannot maintain or improve market share. If products are difficult for customers to use or do not meet their needs, or if sales people don't understand products well, or, especially, if support service is inadequate, market share will be lost. In short, progress in this area is important because service represents a major business opportunity. Customers want a personal touch, and IBM is striving to be not only high tech but "high touch" as well. At IBM, we use the same process management discipline that applies to high technology for meeting special customer requirements. However, decisions cannot be made in isolation. First of all, the customer must be a player on the team. Secondly, strategic knowledge within the company cannot be isolated in one person or staff: Executives must develop cross-functional expertise to understand how a decision by one department affects others. IBM is moving in this direction of executive development, but we must do more.

Part IV
Quality as Management Process and Business Strategy

Transferring Customer Needs to Nuclear Power Operations: FPL'S Policy Deployment Process

Joseph W. Dickey
Vice President of Nuclear Operations
Florida Power & Light Company

Florida Power & Light (FPL) is the nation's fifth-largest investor-owned electric utility in terms of customers served. We have nearly 3 million customers and supply power to roughly half of Florida's 12 million residents. Last year, about 28 percent of that power came from nuclear energy generated from our four nuclear plants.

At FPL, nuclear operations and our Quality Improvement Program (QIP) go hand in hand. FPL's commitment to quality improvement is such that we no longer view QIP as merely a program: QIP is how we operate the company, the way we do business. That attitude is a necessity because times have changed. A few years ago, most of our customers didn't really care if the power went off for a second or two now and then. Chances are, they didn't even know when it went off. Today, a split-second power outage seldom goes unnoticed. The tiniest blip can cause computer screens to go blank, digital clocks to go blink, and our customers to become very upset. QIP was created to serve and satisfy the customer. It's that simple.

The modern American consumer is more mature, more educated, more affluent, more vocal, and more demanding than ever before. QIP is the process we have developed over the last six years to help us meet the reasonable needs and expectations of our customers. The "customer" in this context is not just the person who pays the electric bill. For FPL, the customer includes such groups as stockholders, the Public Service Commission, the Nuclear Regulatory Commission, and even our fellow employees.

The first indication that quality improvement could make a dramatic difference in our operations came during the construction of our last nuclear unit in the late 1970s and early 1980s. An emphasis on quality techniques helped us complete St. Lucie Unit II in the industry-record time of six years, at a savings of some $600 million. After spending more than a year and a half studying what others were doing in the area of quality improvement, we formally introduced QIP throughout the company in 1981.

43

LIBRARY ST. MARY'S COLLEGE

The tools of QIP are provided in three primary areas:

(1) Quality improvement teams were introduced in 1982. By the end of 1987, more than 8,000 of our 14,000 employees had taken part in team activities.

(2) "Quality in Daily Work" (QIDW) at the management level means establishing top-priority jobs. At other levels, it means improving how the job is done—improving the job process. QIDW helps our employees answer two very basic questions: "How do you know if you're doing a good job?" And, "How do you know if you're doing the right job?" QIDW relies on indicators. Performance indicators are established for each job and those indicators are tracked by the individual doing the job. The worker is his own quality control.

(3) Policy deployment, a management process, was established as a part of QIP in 1984. It allows us to discover our priorities and encourages new and innovative ideas in the way we do business.

Of these three, policy deployment sounds the most abstract and removed from FPL's activities and results. But that process does relate to nuclear operations and, ultimately, to customer satisfaction. Policy deployment helps us determine where we're going and how best to get there. It's basically a planning process that focuses on a small number of priority areas, which then become corporate mid-term goals to be met in five to seven years.

When we established policy deployment, we also established this corporate vision: "During the next decade, we want to become the best-managed electric utility in the United States and an excellent company overall and be recognized as such." Policy deployment was one of the major tools we chose to accomplish those goals.

Input in the form of performance indicators to point us toward the proper priorities is vital, but equally important is the creative input of our employees. Twice each year, managers from all areas of the company meet in what we call situation conferences, or "sitcons." These meetings bring the managers up to date on company plans and allow them to participate actively in the goal-setting process with ideas of their own. From these sitcons come our mid-term goals, which generally number no more than four and are very broad. The goal of achieving customer satisfaction is a good example of that.

The next step of policy deployment is to establish short-term goals that relate directly to the mid-term goals. These are tactical plans that are expected to show results in one to two years. While the mid-term corporate goals tell us what we've got to do to reach our long-term goals, the short-term corporate goals tell us how we're going to do it.

Last year, a total of ten short-term goals were established. The nuclear energy department is directly responsible for three of those goals: improving the public perception of nuclear safety; improving regulatory performance; and continuing to emphasize safe, reliable, and efficient operation of our nuclear power plants. Our progress in the third of these goals illustrates how policy deployment works with the QIP.

One measure of safe, reliable, and efficient operation is nuclear plant reliability. We looked at the performance of our nuclear units over the past four years and found that, although we had operated well above the industry average, there was still plenty of room for improvement. Another indicator showed us that of a total of 1,772 unavailable days for four units during the four-year period, nearly 1,200 were unplanned. We had experienced 670 days off line due to refueling outage extensions and 503 days off line because of other unplanned outages.

Such indicators led us to establish a specific mid-term plan for the nuclear energy department, to improve unit reliability by concentrating on the indicator of unplanned days off line. Policy deployment projects were established at both our Turkey Point and St. Lucie plants to address the matter of unit reliability. At St. Lucie, of 562 unplanned days off line, 74 percent were the result of refueling outage extensions—nuclear refueling operations that simply took longer than we had expected. Nearly 400 of those days came about because of a one-time occurrence of a single major internal reactor repair, the cause of which has been removed. Other unplanned outages, the result of a number of factors over which we had more control, accounted for 146 days off line. It was on those unplanned outages, concentrated on Unit II, that we decided to focus our attention.

A further year-by-year comparison indicated a clear trend of increased unavailability, especially Unit II, which had 58 unplanned days off line in 1985. The situation there appeared to be, in statistical terminology, out of control. These operations led us to set a specific target at St. Lucie: to reduce the unplanned days off line at Unit II to 30 days or less, a reduction of some 50 percent.

Through additional indicators, we learned what had to be done to meet such a goal. We noticed that more than half of the unplanned days off line were the result of failures by a reactor coolant pump. Another indicator showed a comparison of the causes of pump failure: High vibration of the motor shaft and failure of the pump seal were responsible for 92 percent of the failures. Thus, to achieve our target, we needed to eliminate both problems.

Through the QIP analysis process, quality improvement teams were organized and the root causes of each of the problems were found. Countermeasures were developed and an action plan implemented. In the 24 months since the countermeasures went into effect, there have been zero unplanned days off line as a result of coolant pump failures. We have performed even better than our target, and the trend of increased unplanned days off line has been reversed.

With policy deployment, we had started with a relatively general corporate plan, and with the help of indicators, we were able to come with specific solutions to help meet a much broader goal. And furthermore, while it may not be immediately obvious, the policy deployment accomplishments of the nuclear energy department are directly related to customer satisfaction. While many of our rate-paying customers may not even be aware of whether or not our nuclear units are in operation, the reduction of unplanned days off line affects them in a very sensitive area—their pocketbooks.

Nuclear generation requires the lowest fuel cost to our customers. Producing energy with nuclear fuel costs about 70 percent less than with oil or gas. The dollar savings gained in maximizing our nuclear energy output—savings that go directly to the customers—are significant. In addition, by increasing availability and reliability, we're cutting down on operating and maintenance expenses, and part of those benefits go to yet another group of customers—our shareholders.

By running our nuclear operations more efficiently, we're helping to satisfy the requirements of the Public Service Commission and the Nuclear Regulatory Commission. We're also helping to satisfy our "internal" customers—our co-workers. Those working in our fossil plant units, for example, are delighted to have the time available to perform preventive maintenance, time they might not have if our nuclear units were not running so efficiently.

In 1986, Florida Power & Light was fortunate enough to be named winner of the Edison Award, the highest honor given within the electric utility industry. In the award presentation, the quality improvement program was singled out as the most significant contribution in effectively serving our customers.

AT&T's Full-Stream Quality Architecture

Laurence C. Seifert
Vice President, Engineering, Manufacturing, and Production Planning
American Telephone and Telegraph Company

We believe our customers view quality as their entitlement from AT&T. The association in customers' minds between quality and a firm's name is a company's most valuable asset, and, to a great extent, AT&T enjoys such an association. Our quality policy makes a two-fold promise. Not only do we promise our customers products and services that meet their expectations for quality, we also promise that we'll pursue continuous quality improvement through practices that enable each and every employee to do the right job the first time or do it better each time.

A quality architecture must encompass every work process. We use the term architecture because, although our quality program includes an organization, it's not a bureaucracy. We haven't added people, we've simply linked them in a communication structure that helps every business group in the company do two things effectively: communicate its requirements to the organizations that supply it; and be more responsive to the requirements of its customers.

By customers I do not mean only *end* customers. The process model of quality at AT&T works on the premise that everyone has customers—either inside or outside the company. Everybody in our firm participates in achieving and improving quality in his or her own business process. And every business organization participates in the quality architecture through formal communications links to supplier and customer organizations. For example, in Chicago, we have a support services organization that is responsible for word processing and reprographics and that wanted to improve its accuracy and efficiency. So, the people at this organization adopted the time-proven methods of statistical process control. First, they outlined their processes on flow charts to be sure they understood them. Then, they took a structured brainstorming approach called cause-and-effect analysis to identify potential sources of waste and rework. Next, they established what was critical to measure over the long term and then put these measures on process control charts.

The results: a five-fold improvement in typing accuracy and a halving of turnaround time in reprographics. They also found that better communication with their customers carried most of the potential for gains and continued gains.

47

For example, ~~they~~ put the typists in direct contact with customers when instructions were complex. Now there are fewer misunderstandings, fewer mistakes, and less rework. With the work coming to the customers faster, more deadlines are being met. And that translates into customer satisfaction and a better business operation for ~~AT&T.~~

You could say that this team fixed its process but fix isn't quite the right word. ~~They~~ did more: By analyzing thoroughly their process and relations to suppliers and customers, ~~they~~ ensured that improvements didn't come at the expense of performance somewhere else in the organization. The ~~Chicago~~ team also set the stage for continuous process improvement by maintaining process control charts. In this manner deviations can be detected and remedied as they occur, ideally before customer complaints arise.

At ~~AT&T,~~ our quality architecture is being superimposed over the full stream of business activities that drive production and deliver products and services to customers because we believe advances in manufacturing aren't enough. Most of our people work in finance and accounting, in sales and services, in our network operations, and in a growing number of information-processing and administrative functions. These are white-collar workers, not blue-collar workers.

Another large grouping is in R&D organizations, notably AT&T Bell Laboratories; I call these our no-collar workers. Such people are coming to be called, and I use the term reluctantly, "knowledge workers" or "information workers"—people who control the quality of streams of information. These streams flow into a business from customers and the external environment, then flow through a business from product development to manufacturing and distribution, and flow out in the form of sales effort and service follow up.

Unfortunately, although the white-collar sector of industry is growing, its efficiency has not met our needs. Information automation, for example, has not raised white-collar quality or productivity to any great extent. While that is not good news, it implies that white-collar activities present us with a major opportunity. The drive for white-collar quality will enhance the wealth-generating capacity of all workers, including the cadres of information workers who are a driving force in productivity. Fortunately, based on experience with quality management in manufacturing, we have the tools to bring quality management into every corner of our operations.

The recent U. S. Bureau of Labor Statistics report, *Projections 2000,* suggests that the U.S. labor force will expand by nearly 21 million jobs between now and the year 2000. The projected rate of economic growth, however, outpaces the rate of labor force growth. So, productivity growth must make up a good portion of the difference. The forecasted labor force shortage is another opportunity to use available people more productively. Quality improvement among the white-collar workforce will help generate the needed rise in productivity.

In 1985, ~~AT&T~~ began to struggle with strategic quality issues involving white-collar and information-worker processes. We saw that better links between our product developers and manufacturing operations would be the key to producing the designs more effectively. By making use of existing quality experience in manufacture, AT&T has moved into "design for manufacturability."

Design for manufacturability refers to responsive manufacturing processes that "forgive" design deficiencies and to robust product designs that are forgiving of tolerances found in manufacturing processes. Design for manufacturability pleases customers by assuring built-in quality, which also controls costs by maximizing manufacturing yields.

Recent successes in our design for manufacturability have resulted from a structured approach to a process, namely the "product-realization process." Last year, for example, we introduced a new subscriber line carrier. At the very outset of planning for this product, we formed a New Product Introduction Team made up of designers, systems specialists, manufacturing people from the different operations and manufacturing sites involved, and test and quality staff. And we paid close attention to the lead customer's requirements.

In the product's first two years, only two significant design changes were needed. A predecessor product required 24 in the same period (and that product itself has been extremely successful). Warranty costs in the first two years were just 2 percent of the earlier product, and initial yields from manufacturing were significantly higher.

Disciplined product realization has come to stay at AT&T. And we'll continue to get good results from it due to new communications links between designers and manufacturers and training activities that make those links work. We're also embarking on an "exchange program" in which design and manufacturing engineers will spend extensive periods in each other's organizations striving to better understand each other's needs.

The implementation of a full-stream architecture has helped AT&T emerge from divestiture as a new company rededicated to continuous quality improvement.

Quality Methods and Business Planning

David F. Colicchio
Region Quality Manager
Hewlett-Packard Company

Focusing on quality isn't really new to Hewlett-Packard, but our perception—what it means, and how it's applied—certainly has changed. Hewlett-Packard's quality evolution underwent three phases over the past 15 years: a growing realization of the importance of quality in competition; the beginnings of our total quality program; and the application of quality methods to planning.

The First Phase

In the mid- to late-1970s, Hewlett-Packard, like many other companies, felt the increased demands of competition in the marketplace. Technology was becoming more of a commodity, and making a superior product was no longer enough. One calculator can only be so much better than another. We had to lower our prices and, in order to do that, we had to lower our internal costs of doing business. A number of our operating business units conducted "cost of quality" studies. And, in every case, we found that our costs of not doing things right the first time were from 25 to 30 percent of our revenues. Based on this finding, our CEO, John Young, set a "stretch" objective in 1979 for the company. He challenged us to improve the reliability of our hardware by tenfold by end-1989.

In response to this challenge, we sent study groups to our joint venture in Japan, Yokogawa Hewlett-Packard (YHP), where astounding gains in quality improvement had been made through total quality control (TQC). YHP had struggled for many years to achieve parity with our domestic operations. In fact, from 1963 until the mid-1970s, by any comparison, they were among our poorest performers. But from 1977, when they first embraced TQC, until 1982 when they won a Deming prize, they turned the situation completely around. Their achievements include:

- A 42 percent reduction in manufacturing costs;
- An R&D-cycle time drop of 52 percent;
- A 193% rise in market share;
- A profit rise of 244 percent.

All these experiences—the forces of competition, the cost of quality, YHP's successes, our goal of a tenfold improvement—helped shape our current understanding of quality. In 1980, Hewlett-Packard launched a company-wide TQC effort.

The Second Phase

In the early 1980s our manufacturing facilities were the first to follow YHP's lead. For example, in an eighteen-month period one of our computer divisions reduced its manufacturing cycle time for printed circuit boards from sixteen days to one day. And by using just-in-time manufacturing techniques, the material goes through the production line so fast that virtually all work-in-progress inventory has been eliminated.

After gaining experience in manufacturing, we shifted our focus to other production environments. The use of TQC in the product repair centers has enabled our U.S. support organization to reduce its repair turnaround time by 25 percent without increasing the size of the workforce. For example, our Roseville, California, computer-support operation is responsible for supplying repair parts and exchange assemblies for all our computers worldwide. Until recently, members of this operation had a less-than-enviable reputation with customers, who are Hewlett-Packard's field sales representatives. Their delivery time just wasn't fast enough. So they used TQC methods to thoroughly analyze their own repair processes and identify what slowed things down. They found that 80 percent of their delivery delays were caused by waiting for just 20 percent of the parts they needed—parts that came from other Hewlett-Packard divisions.

But they didn't point a finger at the guilty divisions. Instead, they put on an educational roadshow that they took around the company. It mapped the entire process of preparing customer orders (or end-user orders) from the customer, to the engineer in our field organization, to the Roseville computer support operation, to the supplying division, back to computer support, and then back to the customer engineers when repaired. This broad, informative picture, with its focus on internal and external customers, convinced the other divisions that they were an integral part of a very large and important process. They are now much faster in sending parts to computer support; they see themselves as part of the same team.

Total quality control also helped our accounts-receivable performance. We have an operation that, in essence, serves as our catalog sales division. It books about 25 percent of all our orders each year, mostly small sales handled over the telephone. In 1984 our overdue collections in this division were $652,000. Management was unhappy, as were the customers whose shipments were put on hold because bills were unpaid. As the Hewlett-Packard credit people dug into the problem via TQC methodology, they turned up some surprising and embarrassing facts. In many cases, customers weren't paying their bills due to our errors—wrong product, wrong address, wrong price, etc. Hewlett-Packard improved its internal processes, dropping overdue receivables to $218,000 within two years. The aggregate results of these kinds of efforts throughout the company are large: overall inventory savings of $475,000 and, a natural spin-off, floor space savings of $200,000, and company-wide savings in accounts receivable of $150,000.

The Third Phase

Despite the favorable results of our early domestic TQC initiative, many of us at Hewlett-Packard began to worry that the initial impact of TQC would die as many programs do. To prevent that we need to keep management involved. For many years, we had prided ourselves on being the first company to put into practice the management principles expressed by the term "management by objectives." But the process of developing and implementing plans is really just that—a process. So it's subject to the same kinds of analysis and improvement as any other process. And this management process needs to be improved, just as any other.

We found that we needed some changes in our planning and implementation process. For example, our annual plans had to become living documents. We needed measurable, clear, and realistic objectives that could be met within a year's time. In addition, we needed implementation plans that were truly capable of driving a change throughout the organization.

So, we began a structured process where objectives, strategies, and measures are hierarchically linked, spanning all functions of the business. This process starts with an annual review—an analytical review of the previous year's objectives and accomplishments. Key issues are then identified and analyzed from the bottom up to determine how much improvement or change is required in the next planning cycle. Extensive, detailed, and structured planning follows, with plans deployed at each level linked with all other plans being developed. A strategy and measure at one level of management will become an objective and goal to the next level down: How a manager wants to accomplish an objective becomes the "what" that has to be done by the next level down.

Finally, the strategies come to life through the detailed implementation plans. Periodic review is essential to the implementation process. Built-in progress checks and reviews verify that the strategies were correct, that implementation is progressing, and that goals will be met. And if not, changes are required. Of course, getting through this process is one step toward the ultimate goal of improved performance. By focusing on improving the process of strategic planning and implementation, we get all managers directly involved. In the future, they will become TQC practitioners.

Part V

Measures of Performance Improvement

Measuring the Quality of Services

John J. Falzon
Senior Vice President
Metropolitan Life Insurance Company

At Met Life, our quest for quality began several years ago. We've learned a lot from others, especially our associates in manufacturing, for they were pioneers in the quality effort. However, we've also had to modify our approach, since we're a services company.

Initial Quality Improvement Efforts

Like many other companies, Met Life began its drive for quality with the introduction of a Quality Steering Committee made up of the heads of major departments throughout the company. This committee provided us with a series of directives that became the foundation of our quality improvement process (QIP). They told us that any program for quality must have a strong customer orientation and that everyone in the company must be involved. They strongly recommended that the entire process be administered through the line organization with minimal staff support and that any process be carried out in a unified way.

Using these directives as guidelines, a process was introduced in 1985 that was designed to alter the way things were being managed and the way work was being done. The new process required every organization to identify the major services being provided and the customers served. Each organization then developed a quality network around the identified services and established performance measures. Organized as teams and using a structured problem-solving technique, they were encouraged to isolate both problems and opportunities and to suggest solutions. From the beginning, the teams were urged to establish challenging goals—especially through open dialogue with their customers, who could give them the most precise evaluation of their performance.

Service Quality Research

At the beginning of 1986, we came across original research by a group of professors from Texas A&M University. The researchers isolated several distinct characteristics of services industries:

(1) Services are intangible and cannot be measured, tested, or verified in advance of sales to assure quality.

(2) Services are heterogeneous, not uniform, because they generally have a high labor content. Performance and evaluation of the service can vary depending on the individual providing the service and the customer who receives it.

(3) For many services, production and consumption are inseparable. In many situations, the customer participates directly in the process, such as getting a haircut, and that involvement becomes critical to the quality of performance.

(4) Services are perishable. They cannot be saved or inventoried.

The researchers concluded that, because of its people-intensive nature, the process of delivering a service is as important as the outcome. In other words, the way a customer is treated in a service transaction can be as important an influence on customer attitude as the actual outcome of the experience. The researchers were able to identify five significant types of factors that influence the overall evaluation of service quality:

(1) *Reliability,* the ability to perform the promised service dependably and accurately;

(2) *Responsiveness,* the willingness to help customers and provide prompt service;

(3) *Tangibles,* physical facilities, equipment, and appearance of personnel;

(4) *Assurance,* the knowledge and courtesy of employees and their ability to convey trust and confidence;

(5) *Empathy,* the caring, individual attention provided to customers.

Each of these five classifications can be expressed as a series of "expectation" statements, which are further refined so that more meaningful customer data can be collected. In line with this approach, the researchers developed a survey that quantifies service performance levels by comparing customer expectations with customer assessments of how well the service provider meets those expectations. The gap between expectation and perceived level of service delivery represents the extent of a service problem. Moreover, the survey was designed within a system that assists management in identifying and isolating problem areas.

The researchers tested their survey in four different services industries. They originally assumed that the better companies on balance were those whose perceived level of delivery consistently *exceeded* the level of their customers' expectations. Instead, their results showed that even the better companies rarely exceeded customers' expectations. These companies merely had a smaller gap.

Applying the Research Results

These results were useful at Metropolitan Life for helping to solve practical business problems. We saw a weakness in the way our teams were engaging in customer dialogue. In many cases, there was a failure to develop the type of customer information that would pinpoint problems and opportunities for improvement. We also found that teams engaged in less quantifiable activities—consulting, training, systems analysis—sometimes had difficulty in developing effectiveness measures that reflected what the customer wanted. So, this research seemed to provide us with a model approach toward developing not only actionable data but also a series of measures that could be tracked over time to determine if progress was being made.

Our initial directive from the Quality Steering Committee was that our quality effort should be line driven, with minimal staff support. Our challenge, as a corporate staff, was thus to communicate the results of this research in an easily understandable way, showing the line organizations how they could apply the principles to their own operations. With the assistance of one of the Texas A&M professors, we structured a special seminar that was delivered to principal officers from all parts of the company in late 1986. Our expectation was that each of the various departments would then survey to quantify their customers' level of satisfaction. Our line areas initially applied this service quality research to their operations in this fashion:

The Policy Issue Team from one of our administrative offices concentrated on improving service to internal customers—the sales managers. In line with the twin challenges of improving customer satisfaction and eliminating extra processing, the team began work in May 1987 to prepare for the "end-of-the-year" crunch—when sales offices experience a final push to meet goals.

The team developed a series of expectation statements, making sure that all five of the service quality dimensions noted in the research were covered. Statements on responsiveness included: "Calling Underwriting will not usually speed my case" and "Electronic mail may get faster action than the phone." In addition to the expectation statements, other questions tested the adequacy of standards the team had established—such as turnaround time for "rush" cases—and the clarity and timeliness of the communications distributed during the previous "year-end" period.

Customer reaction was overwhelming. Eighty-seven percent of the sales managers surveyed responded and the Policy Issue Team became aware of the potential for some rather "painful gaps." The results led the team to institute procedural changes designed to help them meet their customer expectations.

Other changes focused on improving customer perceptions of the service that was already being delivered. For example, the sales offices often used electronic mail for inquiries on case status and then followed up with telephone calls—thereby handling the same case twice, an excellent example of extra processing! Through the survey, the team found that offices were doing this because they were not receiving acknowledgment that their electronic mail messages had been read. Now, a simple acknowledgment lets the field office know its inquiry is being worked on—significantly cutting down on telephone inquiries.

I look forward to seeing the team repeat its survey in early 1988 using perception statements that parallel the expectations statements used in 1987. In this way, its members will be able to see how well the customers perceived the service that had been delivered to them during year-end 1987 and how successful the team had been in anticipating and closing any gaps.

An example from another area of Metropolitan Life represents a pure adaptation of the service quality research. The organization involved is our Electronics Installations Department (EID). EID is an operation of 2,000 employees who provide service to our employees who use EID-supported computer hardware and software.

EID customized the initial service quality survey developed by the Texas A&M team and came up with 32 pairs of expectations/perceptions. A few examples follow:

Assurance

Expectation: All business matters should be dealt with in a confidential manner.

Performance: EID makes a practice of dealing with business matters in a confidential manner.

Responsiveness

Expectation: The availability of the on-line network should meet the customer's business needs.

Performance: The availability of the on-line network provided by EID meets my business needs.

Again, response to the survey was substantial. Of the 292 customers surveyed, 54 percent responded. In analyzing the gaps that existed in terms of each dimension and the specific contributing factors, the department was able to pinpoint its strengths and, even more importantly, its specific opportunities for improvement.

The strengths included physical facilities and equipment, technical expertise, confidentiality, and the personalized care provided by the customer-contact personnel. The areas of opportunity for improvement included soliciting customer feedback, pricing, system response time, communications, training, publications, operating hours, and responsiveness to ad hoc requests.

The immediate results of the survey was EID's 1987 Customer Survey Action Plan. First, feedback of the survey results was sent to the 292 customers who had originally received the survey. Second, customers are being asked to participate in focus groups and to evaluate solutions being proposed by EID's Quality Improvement Teams. Finally, the department plans to repeat the survey in one year to determine the progress it has made in "closing the gaps."

In 1988, the service quality approach will be extended to customers *outside* Met Life. In fact, as part of the annual business planning cycle, all Met Life organizations are required to describe their understanding of customer expectations and the action plans that center on meeting and exceeding those expectations.

Next Steps

One of the greatest satisfactions from our work with the Texas A&M research is that we now have a way to measure quality in the service sector from the customers' perspective. The research postulated a model that not only describes the gap in quality from a customer's perspective but also hypothesizes four types of "gaps" found within service organizations that contribute to customer dissatisfaction:

(1) Management may not truly understand what customer expectations are.

(2) Management may understand the customer's expectations but fail to translate them into the performance standards it establishes for its employees.

(3) Even when specifications match customer expectations, actual delivery may fall short.

(4) A gap may result from communications that may unduly raise customer expectations (the service organization may promise more than it can deliver) or that do not succeed in making customers aware of what is being done for their benefit.

As we look to the future, we hope to gain significant insights into our customers' needs and to go one step further by providing a level of service that will exceed their expectation levels.

Designing a New Family of Measures

Jackie P. Comola
Vice President, White-Collar Productivity
American Productivity Center

Measuring white-collar productivity is critical to a firm's bottom line, but what a burden of responsibility that places on those who must determine what to measure! For example, what happens if the only factor measured is volume or meeting a deadline when what the customer wants is quality? It's important that we measure, but it's also crucial that we assess the right things—those outputs of highest value to our customers. And good measures can also be a tool to channel efforts and reward people for doing the right thing in the right way. How can we ensure that our measures are on the right track? The answer is simple: ask customers and employees. Involve both in establishing a set of meaningful performance indicators.

The White-Collar Dilemma

Some common characteristics of white-collar work make it more difficult to measure than assembly-line production. Many white-collar workers never have contact with the final customer—their customers are internal. White-collar workers such as design engineers, word processing staff, or data processing staff may produce a service or supply knowledge that contributes to the final product. Moreover, their work is often non-repetitive and dependent on what other employees do. All of these considerations make it imperative that the performance measures reflect a set of services provided by a group of workers rather than individual output.

Here are some characteristics to keep in mind when measuring white-collar performance:

- The output encompasses a group of services;
- The customer is internal;
- Communication is critical in determining output;
- Work is interdependent with other functions;
- Much of what's done is non-repetitive.

A work group's performance comprises several dimensions and its value varies in the marketplace, from company to company, and from customer to customer.

It may be more important to one customer to receive information quickly, even if it is incomplete, while to another customer the accuracy of the information may be paramount. The ability to focus on what the customer values is the key—this is the "value added" that differentiates one company's marketplace success from another company's failure.

Obviously, a company has to target its market, but today's environment of accelerated change requires an unprecedented flexibility of resources for shifts in the market service/product mix. The ability to adjust the focus of resources is a benefit of a performance measurement system that includes more than a single criterion. One term for such a multi-dimensional system is a "family of measures." Naturally, there are several kinds of families that can be constructed. The measurement dimensions that seem to cover most of a work group's performance are productivity, quality, timeliness, and effectiveness as perceived by the user. These various families of measures might involve:

Internal Productivity Measures
   —transactions per work hour
   —tests per machine hour
   —weighted reports per scientist
External Productivity Measures
   —post-auditing versus estimate
   —budget
   —comparisons with alternative outside supply
Internal Quality Measures
   —rework
   —errors caught
   —changes required
   —interruptions
   —intermediate failure rates
Effectiveness Perceived by User
   —suitability of product/service
   —complaints, returns, etc.

Expectations can differ and conflicts may occur between internal and external measures of performance and output. The work group can perform at a high level according to an established internal measure but still not meet the expectations and needs of the customer. Volume of output versus quality of output is one such glaring example. Or groups may meet a production goal or a deadline but lose customers because of poor quality. A work group may perform excellent but tardy work, which creates a problem for the group receiving the output.

That is particularly important to consider with white-collar groups that have predominantly internal users. For example, consider a data processing department that, by maximizing its technological resources, has wrecked havoc with the user, who is still processing output manually. The involvement of all three players—supplier, work unit providing a set of services, and users of those services—is the ideal team to develop appropriate measures to manage expectations, reduce conflict, and achieve satisfactory results.

As this implies, performance measures must be perceived as relevant to those who are being measured. One way to ensure that is to involve those being appraised in the development of the measures. Measures can be developed by expert inspection, by management, and through the use of something called nominal group technique (NGT). When NGT is used, teams of employees, management, and users nominate appropriate measures. The steps in the NGT process are:

- Statement of problem
- Individual lists of possible measures
- Round-robin collection of possibilities
- Editing of nominations
- Voting and ranking
- Discussion and consensus

Follow-up steps to develop a measurement system after the NGT sessions include:

- Measures integration
- Weight estimates
- Design of monitor/feedback system

In a continuous performance improvement process called IMPACT (see Box), which we have used with 54 companies, measures development is one of the most critical of the six phases. The measures development phase includes measurement team formation, inventory of current measures, development of measures using NGT, implementation plan, cost check, and feedback. The outcome of this phase is a family of measures for a set of services and a monitoring feedback/correction system.

Here, for example, is a family of measures developed by a team from a computer center:

- Reports/employee hour
- Downtime
- Completion by user deadline
- Re-run time
- On-line response

The measurement system serves as a mechanism to continually examine progress toward meeting strategic goals and toward providing what the users or customers value.

**IMPACT: A Continuing Improvement
Process for Organizational Performance**

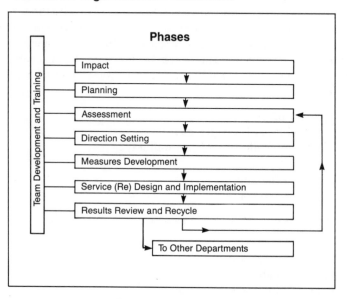

Innovative Methods and Plans in ACTion, IMPACT, is a process organizations use to improve the productivity, quality, and effectiveness of their white collar workforce.

Based on meeting the needs of internal and external customers, IMPACT helps organizations focus effectively on what products and services are necessary and on redesigning work to meet those objectives.

IMPACT Phases

1. *Planning*

The IMPACT process begins with planning. The purpose of planning is to establish a clear understanding of management's expectations and select work groups where the IMPACT process will be implemented. These groups are called "pilot groups." During the planning phase, the organization begins to address the fundamental issues of who will be involved and how the effort will be integrated into the organization.

In IMPACT, several individuals are designated to play key roles. First, a "company liaison" identifies appropriate pilot groups within the company. This individual serves on the IMPACT project steering committee and coordinates the company's overall participation in IMPACT. Often, companies also appoint a "company coordinator" to help facilitate the work and progress of all the pilot work groups involved in IM-

PACT. Within each pilot group, a "pilot manager" is appointed to run the process.

The planning phase involves a number of briefings on the process for key managers and others. The roles of the various participants are identified so that responsibilities are clear. During this phase the company coordinator and pilot group managers receive eight days of intensive leadership and process training to prepare them for their roles in the implementation process.

2. Assessment

The assessment phase is the "Where are we?" phase. Unique to the Center's IMPACT process is the use of surveys and interviews to determine opportunities and areas of priority within each pilot group.

The surveys and interviews explore key relationships and concerns of the pilot group and its suppliers and customers. Participation of suppliers and customers in this effort helps to improve communications and to better identify issues affecting quality and productivity. During this phase, an inventory of current and planned technology is made.

By the end of the assessment phase, services for each pilot group have been identified along with opportunities for improvement. Also, the assessment phase often leads to improved relationships between pilot groups' customers and suppliers.

3. Direction Setting

Direction setting is the "Where do we want to go?" phase. In this phase each pilot group determines its productivity improvement goals. Direction-setting teams typically are formed around key services to establish improvement objectives and an improvement plan. Management approval of the plan and objectives is required.

The major outcomes of this phase are a statement of direction, a statement of services, and improvement objectives.

4. Measures Development

Measurement is the basis for determining the pilot group's progress against objectives. The old cliche, "You can't manage if you can't measure," applies to IMPACT as well.

IMPACT provides a "family of measures" that allows each pilot group to track its progress from "Where are we?" to "Where do we want to go?" The family of measures provides the pilot group the tools it needs to measure progress, to give feedback, and to know when to take additional corrective actions. In addition, current measures are inventoried and used along with new measures. It is most effective if both the customer and supplier participate in this phase.

5. *Service (Re)Design and Implementation*

After key services have been identified, objectives established, and measurements developed, service delivery systems are examined and improved.

Typical activities include mapping current delivery and service systems and identifying critical process points and interfaces. Methods of improvement are explored by the pilot group, such as reduced handling, reduced steps, reorganization of inputs, streamlined decision making, new technology requirements, and changing roles and responsibilities.

A key objective of this phase is to gain employee acceptance and participation as well as ownership in the redesign. The redesigned services are linked directly to the pilot group's objectives for improvement as established in earlier phases.

6. *Results Review and Recycle*

The objectives of this phase are to determine the extent to which progress has taken place, to take steps to ensure the improvements will be sustained, to encourage the use of IMPACT as a continuous improvement tool, and to plan for expansion of IMPACT into other areas.

The core activities are to measure results, do pre/post-comparisons, and document the level of performance improvements achieved by the work groups.

Customer Perspective as a Competitive Weapon

E. Neal Trogdon
Executive Vice President
The First National Bank of Chicago

In today's competitive environment, total customer service and product excellence are critical to the long-term success of the financial services industry. Our business requires dozens, sometimes hundreds of steps, procedures, checks, and balances be performed within a certain critical time period to satisfy the customer. Adding to these pressures, competition is always growing. Foreign financial institutions are relying on price cutting to provide full-scale global financial services to low-risk customers.

In addition, banks are becoming less important as a source of funds. Major corporations, for example, can readily raise funds in global debt, equity, and commercial paper markets to meet borrowing needs. (However, venture capital, mezzanine funds, and syndication efforts used by banks in corporate reorganizations and leveraged buy-outs offset this trend.) Finally, U.S. financial market regulations continue to evolve: Nontraditional participants (commercial banks) can and will engage in securities underwriting, insurance, and real estate.

Strategic Focus on Quality

To better respond to our customers, First Chicago organized to provide customers added value through relationship management, product excellence, and greater commitment to customer service and relationship continuity. We realized that in order to be competitive we had to carve out a "niche" for ourselves in the marketplace. So, we turned to our customers and started asking them questions about quality, customer service, price, competitors, and innovation. Our definition of quality is what our customers say it is. In the beginning, we asked two very important questions:

- What do you consider good quality features of banking products? (We wanted to make sure we were doing the right things right.)
- What do you consider good quality in the delivery of those features?

Case Study: Lock-Box Services

Both conviction and a high level of investment—in people, training, data processing systems, and rewards—drive our efforts. Along with this goes a willingness and ability to seek and anticipate customers' needs. That strategic direction is illustrated by the history of one of our core cash management products—itself the result of a customer need over 40 years ago. In 1947, First Chicago was the first bank in the United States to open a lock-box service, which it did for one of its customers, RCA Corporation. That operation consisted of one employee, a typewriter, an adding machine, and an annual budget of $10,000. The unit was part of the mail department.

To clarify briefly, lock-box processing is carried out both between corporations and individuals and between two companies. For example, if ABC Corporation sends an invoice to XYZ Corporation, XYZ will then mail its payment, which is received at a post office box and taken to the bank. The envelope is opened by a person in the lock-box area who removes the check and invoice copy. The amounts are verified, the payment is recorded, and the amount credited to ABC Corporation's account. Finally, the check is processed. Often, information is transmitted to the bank's customer several times each day.

By 1964, First Chicago recognized lock-box service as a distinct product with great marketing potential, and a separate operating unit was formed by the early 1980s. In 1983, First Chicago introduced its wholly-owned-and-operated network of processing sites (Charlotte, North Carolina; Chicago, Illinois; Dallas, Texas; Pasadena, California; and Newark, New Jersey). By 1986, First Chicago had established itself as the dominant provider of nationwide lock-box services. We now have over 2,300 active accounts which generate about 27 million items annually, with a value of $123 billion. Our quality ratio of one error per 9,000 items processed is three times better than the industry standard.

Ensuring Customer Satisfaction

Four processes are especially important for ensuring customer satisfaction: (1) Performance Measurement, (2) Specialized Service, (3) Employee Involvement, and (4) Reward and Recognition.

We base the first process, performance measurement, on what the customers have said is important to them. In lock-box services, for example, some of the customer concerns were:

- How much was collected?
- When are funds available?
- Who paid for what?

To gauge our performance on the first question, we measure how many times the incorrect deposit information was given to customers (see Chart 1). On the second question, we measure the dollars deposited by 9:30 a.m., a critical time for making investment decisions (see Chart 2). To assess who paid, we measure how many times we report remittance information incorrectly (see Chart 3). Senior management reviews these key performance measurements weekly.

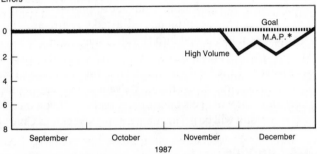

Chart 1

Wholesale Lockbox:
Automated Transmission Errors

Errors

Goal
M.A.P.*
High Volume

September · October · November · December

1987

*Minimal Acceptance Performance

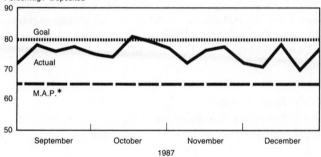

Chart 2

Wholesale Lockbox:
Dollars Deposited Before 9:30 a.m.

Percentage Deposited

Goal
Actual
M.A.P.*

September · October · November · December

1987

*Minimal Acceptance Performance

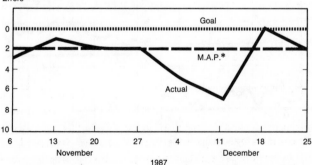

Chart 3

Lockbox
Data Key Errors—Incidents Reported

Errors

Goal
M.A.P.*
Actual

6 · 13 · 20 · 27 · 4 · 11 · 18 · 25

November · December

1987

*Minimal Acceptance Performance

All in all, 700 customer-sensitive issues are measured and analyzed at First Chicago. These issues fall into the categories of accuracy, timeliness, and responsiveness to customers. Minimal acceptance performance (MAP) standards and goal lines are set by each strategic business unit and approved by senior management. MAPs and goal lines are continually adjusted upward, and the calculation of management bonuses is tied into the attainment of MAPs and goals.

When MAP is not met, plans for corrective action must be reported. Management from other areas of the bank attend the meetings. Customers and vendors are invited and encouraged to attend. We've learned that people respect what you inspect and that what gets measured gets done. If you measure, analyze, and correct, the result will be performance improvement, as Chart 4 shows.

Decentralized Service

Developing specialized service is the second quality process we use to ensure customer satisfaction. We changed our structure from a centralized customer-service approach—in which our reps had limited knowledge of a large variety of products—to a customer service unit within each of our product areas. We created product specialists and put them in contact with the ultimate product specialist—the customer.

A third quality process is employee involvement, which places problem identification and ownership at the right level. It also improves communication with management. Our successes have been due to the involvement and ingenuity of employees.

Finally, we have numerous reward and recognition programs:

- Monthly Team Awards
- Sales/Customer Service Excellence Club
- Business Unit Programs:
  "Walk an Extra Mile for a Customer"
  "Error-Free Performers"

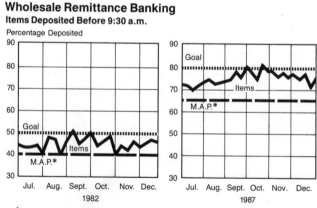

Chart 4

Wholesale Remittance Banking
Items Deposited Before 9:30 a.m.

* Minimal Acceptance Performance

We also give "samples"; that is, we link financial rewards to performance through salary, special incentive bonus, or shares. All of these quality process- es reflect our corporate mission and commitment:

Mission
The mission of First Chicago Corporation is to be the the premier bank hold- ing company in the Midwest with a reputation for excellence in serving cus- tomers nationwide and throughout the world.

Commitment
- The customer is First Chicago's highest priority.
- We are strategically driven as an institution.
- Teamwork is the way First Chicago works.
- Our people are the key to our success.

Customer-Driven Quality

Thomas P. Enright
Manager, Quality Control Office
Casting Division, Ford Motor Company

Ford Motor Company is made up of three operations: Ford Automotive Group, Ford Financial Services Group, and Diversified Products Operations. The Casting Division is part of the Automotive Group of Diversified Products Operations, which has nine different divisions. We employ about 7,000 people and our products include engine blocks, cylinder heads, pistons, other iron and aluminum cast parts, and forged steel connecting rods.

The economic turbulence of the late 1970s and early 1980s was the catalyst that accelerated changes at Ford and in the entire automotive industry. Internally, we instituted a comprehensive participative-management and employee-involvement program in 1979. The program applies to employees at all levels and is designed to support continuous improvement through participation.

In line with internal changes, the Casting Division recognized the need for customer input. Six basic elements make up the arm-in-arm program with our customers:

(1) Developing common goals to identify opportunities for improvement in quality and manufacturing processes.

(2) Maintaining timely and effective communications at all levels.

(3) Establishing and preserving close customer ties.

(4) Launching new products in conjunction with our customer plants and using joint launch teams.

(5) Reviewing product feasibility with the "upfront" participation of both product engineers and manufacturers. This ensures that product designs and manufacturing processes will be compatible.

(6) Providing our customers with products that are best-in-class quality.

These customer ties and programs have gathered momentum and continue to generate mutual benefits and customer satisfaction. To formalize Ford's position regarding continuous quality improvement, a revised quality system standard, which we call "Q101," was developed in 1983 for all Ford suppliers. Q101 has benefited from constructive input from many of our suppliers and is designed to provide:

- A better understanding of the ability of statistical process control to improve quality and productivity.
- The quality standards and guidelines for internal and external suppliers.
- An introduction to the Q-l Preferred Quality Supplier Program, in which suppliers are awarded a preferred status for outstanding quality performance. Currently, 50 percent of Ford's purchased dollar volume is from suppliers with a Q-l rating.

A New Quality Approach

Ford's "Total Quality Excellence" program, completed and introduced in 1985, emphasizes the importance of quality in everything we do, with the goal of achieving superior external and internal customer satisfaction levels. The Total Quality Excellence program includes an achievement award as recognition for a high level of continuous improvement in the quality of products and services provided to Ford customers. This award goes beyond the scope of Ford's highly successful Q1 Preferred Quality Award by honoring the top echelon of Q1 suppliers. Its recipients are further rewarded with ongoing partnership and purchasing decisions.

Our total quality excellence process (see Chart 1) is one of the primary tools we use to ensure continuous improvement in all areas of our business. An example of this program in action is our switchover from a *detection* to a *prevention* system of quality control. In the past, we used the traditional detection method of controlling quality with 100 percent inspection—sorting the "OKs" from the "not-Oks" for scrap or rework. This after-the-fact detection system was both too costly and too late for effective process control.

Now the Casting Division uses a prevention method that has statistical process control integrated into the manufacturing process (see Chart 2). This type of

---

Chart 1

CASTING DIVISION
THE TOTAL QUALITY EXCELLENCE PROCESS

- FOCUSES ON CUSTOMER REQUIREMENTS AND CONTINUOUS IMPROVEMENT FOR ALL PRODUCTS AND SERVICES

- INVOLVES THE ENTIRE WORKFORCE IN TEAM-ORIENTED IMPROVEMENT EFFORTS

- USES PROBLEM SOLVING AND STATISTICAL TECHNIQUES

- MEASURES PROGRESS MADE IN EACH AREA AGAINST A BASELINE

- *WORKS TOWARD THE OVERALL VISION OF THE DIVISION*

Chart 2

QUALITY APPROACH

DETECTION	**PREVENTION**
• INSPECTION	• STATISTICAL METHODS AND PROCESS CONTROL
• CONFORMANCE TO SPECIFICATIONS	• REDUCING VARIATION IN PROCESS OUTPUT
• ORGANIZATION/TRADITIONAL	• ORGANIZATION/PARTICIPATIVE
• MEET CUSTOMER NEEDS	• EXCEED CUSTOMER EXPECTATIONS
• *SOLVING PROBLEMS USING DESIGNED EXPERIMENTS*	• *SOLVING PROBLEMS USING TRADITIONAL METHODS*

---

in-line control provides us with constant, effective feedback—a key item in the defect-prevention mode of manufacturing. With statistical process control in place, fewer inspectors are required; those who remain are integrated into production. The unprogressive goal of simply meeting the needs of our customers is being replaced with the idea of exceeding customer expectations.

We have also replaced our traditional method of problem solving with the experimental design technique developed in the 1920s by an English mathematician, R.A. Fisher, and adapted and introduced in the Japanese automotive industry in the 1960s. We adopted this technique in 1984, and it has been very valuable in resolving chronic problems that had eluded our efforts. Whereas the traditional problem-solving techniques usually allow for the evaluation of only one characteristic at a time, experimental design provides for the full evaluation of all major process variables and their interaction, which is very important in the casting process. Over 100 experimental design studies have been completed throughout the division, and we have achieved major quality improvements in every case.

A primary indicator of quality at the Casting Division is first-time capability, or FTC—the percent of our castings or forgings that are processed through our customer plants without rejection or rework. It is the goal of all production casters and forgers to attain consistent 100 percent FTC levels on all products they supply to their customers.

In December 1986, we decided to apply experimental design thinking to FTC. We started 1986 with an FTC rate of 98.8 percent, which was considered excellent by industry standards. Initially, we worked on the problem using the standard "one-at-a-time experimentation" approach to determine the root cause. For example, a process variable such as the temperature of the molten metal was adjusted based on past experience, with the results then evaluated and applied. Using this method, our FTC increased to 99.4 percent by year end.

That was quite good. However, as metal casting processes have a wide variety of process variables, we found this problem-solving method slow. So, in December 1986, we applied experimental design to the problem and involved all persons in the plant who could provide input for the experiment. These were the steps:

(1) *Brainstorming.* Each brainstorming session is intended to foster a spirit of teamwork and to provide all attendees with an opportunity to "buy into" the solution of the problem.

One product of such sessions is the identification of all the process variables thought to be be relevant to the problem. In our case, 42 variables were identified by the group. After studying this input, the group then chose seven items as most relevant to the problem.

(2) *Designing the experiment.* Experiment designs are chosen from a book of established design standards. Our case required a seven-variable design to handle the two levels of operating parameters.

(3) *Organizing the experiment.* Each of the eight runs required 700 castings to be made. All affected departments (production, quality control, melting, tooling, etc.) were involved in running the experiment and following the castings through the customer's machine plant to determine the first-time capability of each individual run.

(4) *Determining the "best" operating pattern.* This decision was based on the results of the experiments and a response table (see Table 1). The columns identify the results of all castings in the experiment in terms of

Table 1.

3.8L PISTON SHRINK STUDY

RESPONSE TABLE/FTC %

PROCESS PARAMETER	MEAN RESPONSES FOR	
	LEVEL 1	LEVEL 2
MOLD TEMPERATURE	99.6%	99.2%
DOWNSPRUE RISER	*100%*	98.8%
METAL TEMPERATURE	99.2%	99.6%
MOLD COATING APPLICATION	*99.9%*	99.0%
RISER DESIGN	99.1%	99.4%
MOLD DESIGN	99.0%	*99.9%*
MACHINE CYCLE	99.4%	99.1%

FTC; from these data we determined the recommended operating pattern. The new operating levels of the process variables included the three that are in italics. These were the most important to control quality. The operating levels for the other variables were set at levels of lowest cost.

(5) *Confirming the results of the experiment.* To verify our new operating process levels, we conducted a confirmation run, the last step in our designed experiment process.

The following week we completed the necessary revisions to the casting molds and arranged our processes to accommodate our new operating parameters, which were based on the experiment's results. Our performance for the balance of 1987 showed an increase in FTC to a consistent level of just under 100 percent—a quantum improvement in performance by the plant team.

To sum up, we are convinced that the education and training programs we have in place in the Casting Division are critical to assuring our continued success and growth. We now budget 20 times more for education and training than we did in 1980. Overall, our first-time capability as a division increased from 92.3 percent in 1982 to 98.3 percent in 1987—and we project continued improvement.

Part VI
Managing Quality in the Delivery of Services and Products

LIBRARY ST. MARY'S COLLEGE

Improving Hospital Quality: The Voice of the Customer

Paul B. Batalden, M.D.
Vice President for Medical Care
Hospital Corporation of America

The way we think about medicine today is changing. Before the year 1700 the best result that a physician could hope for was patient care; that has been labeled the "Samaritan" tradition of medicine. About 1750 we saw the introduction of empirical science and for the next 200 years there was a blending of the Samaritan and the scientific traditions. With the introduction of this second tradition in medical care, we saw the definition of the best result change. It became scientifically established as diagnosis and treatment. This is the view that governed the training of most physicians in practice today.

About 1980, I believe, a third tradition emerged. Some call it "cost effectiveness," but I prefer "social accountability." To me it means that people are asking different questions about health care. On an individual basis, it was customary to simply say, "Thank you," at the end of the transaction. Now it's "why?" before "thank you." I think that the definition of the best result has changed to "diagnosis and treatment at best value."

The Context of Quality Improvement

In searching for a theory on which to base the measurement and improvement of quality for today's medicine, we're fortunate to be able to benefit from important work in the quality process field. Of particular relevance is Deming's "cycle for continuous improvement." It begins at the twelve o'clock position with the design of goods, products, or services. At three o'clock is the manufacture of those products or services in accord with design specifications. At six o'clock is placing those goods or services in the marketplace. At the nine o'clock position is obtaining customer judgments of performance and quality under conditions of use, and then inserting those judgments into the redesign of service, product, or good.

At Hospital Corporation of America (HCA) our quality-improvement efforts are grounded in our mission, which is to attain international leadership in the health-care field, provide excellence in health care, improve the standards of health care in the communities in which we operate, provide superior facilities and needed services, enable physicians to best serve the needs of their patients, and generate measurable benefits for the company, medical staff, employee, investor, and, most importantly, the patient. To us, that represents value-driven, quality health care.

Hospitals, like other organizations, have more than one customer, and if we take the Deming cycle for continuous improvement and apply it to the health field, it would look like this: At twelve o'clock is design best-value hospital and health-care services. At three o'clock deliver those services according to the design specs. (Traditionally, our quality assurance activities focused on and measured the twelve o'clock to three o'clock portion of the cycle.) Then at six o'clock, offer those services, and then take patient, physician, and payer (i.e., employers and their agents) judgments of quality and use them to assist in the redesign and improvement of services.

The Voices for Improvement

The voice of the patient/customer is especially important in our cycle. Over the past two years, my colleagues at HCA, along with experts at the Rand Corporation, and at the Harvard School of Public Health, have been at work developing a method to regularly and reliably measure patient views of hospital performance. We developed this system with the assumption, consistent with the third age of medicine, that patients were capable of giving us feedback about much more than we had traditionally sought.

It became clear to us that patients could judge whether their care was personalized and seemed technically competent. If they've been on orange pills and suddenly get a green one, they know that something has changed. They realize that if the IVs routinely run dry, there's something wrong; patients can judge technical competence. They know whether their questions were answered and if services were readily accessible and available, when the call light was answered and when it wasn't. They can tell you whether they were comfortable and secure in the hospital environment, whether the food was palatable, warm, or cold. They can assess whether the outcomes of care met with their expectations.

If you tally up that list and compare it to what we've customarily asked patients, you realize how trivially we've treated them in the past. In short, we realize that patients are in a position to give us low-cost, reliable feedback about hospital care that we can't get from any other source.

If you're concerned with the continuous improvement of an institution you must begin to focus management's attention on the use of longitudinal data and compare the performance of that institution over time. CEOs must know how to use this information. If they're illiterate in this respect, it won't help. In the early days of this system, some of our administrators reported that they actually used the information to refocus the energy of an entire hospital around quality improvement and a commitment to excellence. They were able to:

- Center the attention of the hospital department heads around patient judgment;

- Organize multidisciplinary teams of hospital leaders assigned to redesign the hospital services to better meet the patients' needs and expectations;
- Use the information to systematically identify and recognize areas of excellence within a hospital and to reduce the lead time for pinpointing services that need improvement;
- Use the information to help employees begin the work of defining quality in customer terms.

In short, this system to listen to and use the voice of the patient/customer has helped our leaders focus on and manage the process of quality improvement in their hospitals. We're just starting this process, but we're very excited about it and expect to implement it in about 75 of our hospitals by the end of this year.

The Marriott Strategy: Unparalleled Standards, Exceptional Service

John W. Herold
Vice President
Marriott Hotels-Resorts

Marriott is not only a chain of hotels, it's also the largest airline catering company in the United States, and a major provider of meals in hospitals and office buildings. We also run Roy Rogers restaurants, Bob's Big Boy restaurants, and restaurants and gift shops in airports around the country. We are a large and rapidly growing company. We have achieved this by providing the highest quality service facilities and by constantly paying attention to all the details of our business.

The goal that we've set for ourselves is "unparalleled standards, exceptional services." Right now Marriott Corporation is the seventh largest employer in the United States, according to *Fortune* magazine. We employ over 220,000 employees, and each week there are millions of interactions between these employees and our customers.

As you can imagine, the most difficult part of our business is managing these employee/customer interactions. Mr. Bill Marriott, Senior, founded the company with the basic philosophy that, "If we take good care of our employees, the employees will take care of the customer." He also believed "each employee should have a guarantee of fair treatment," which means the right to take up a grievance through the organization and eventually to Mr. Marriott himself, if necessary.

We break these principles into three basic areas: hiring, training, and monitoring of all employees. Hiring seems simple and yet is often where people fall down in the service industry. Our system is designed to hire people with the right personality and service attitude. We don't care about their experience or about any other issue. We believe we can teach the other things, but we can't teach personality. We can provide training, give them the technical skills, and do all the other things that are necessary with the other programs.

The New York Marriott Marquis is probably the most dramatic example of the process we go through. That hotel has about 2,000 employees and in order to find them, we interviewed 50,000 people. By the time an employee was hired at the Marquis, he or she had gone through five personal interviews. You can imagine the money and the organization that takes, but sifting through 50,000 people left us with the 2,000 that we really feel are the right people, in the right location, with the right attitude.

Training

Once you hire the right employees, you make sure they can provide the service that everybody wants. At the Marriott Marquis, once we hired the 2,000 people, we then put them through our orientation and training program. Orientation takes several weeks. Every member of the executive committee, the five or six executives operating each hotel, must devote half a day to that program a week, speak to all the new employees, and impress upon them the importance of our goals and philosophy.

We use all the training tools available today. We have interactive video that lets employees work on individual computer screens so they can answer questions, deal with the different issues, and role-play. By the time an employee goes on the floor, he or she has gone through a large number of simulated problem situations. There are also standard customer-service training modules that they go through.

Once employees complete this orientation program, we don't just throw them into a job. We have a "buddy system," in which each employee is helped by an experienced employee who knows the ropes. This employee, for example, shows him or her where the locker room is or how to get to the cafeteria. More importantly, they work side by side in the technical part of their jobs. We make sure that the new employees are fully versed in their job, whether it be working a computer or waiting on a table, before they're on their own.

Another significant part of the program is the training of the entry-level management. We have roughly ten employees per manager in our organization. That manager is generally young, lacking in experience, with less developed managerial skills than people farther up in the organization. We spend a good deal of time with these new managers in training programs to make sure they're well equipped for their future positions.

The fundamental tool that we use is called our individual development (ID) program. When a manager is hired, he or she is given a book, along with the orientation in Washington, covering a specific job in detail. It includes clearly designed exercises on topics such as interviewing that are to be completed at each individual's pace. This ID program takes an average of two to three months—a major commitment of time and effort. He or she uses this manual in conjunction with a "counselor," who works on the technical parts of the tasks, and an "advisor," who guides the individual through the managerial sections. We want to be sure that the young manager has the skills necessary to succeed.

Monitoring

The third part of the program is monitoring. We need to know whether we're successful, if we're doing a good job, and how customers feel about our company. The fundamental system we use is the Guest Service Index (GSI)—the little form in hotel room that says, "We care. Please fill out this form." That form is the foundation of our system. Each is sent to Washington to be processed. The ones that mention problems are immediately returned to the site of origin. The rest are sent back after they've been reviewed by our consumer relations department.

Fortunately, Marriott averages about 90 percent positive comments even though this tool was originally designed to handle problems. We use this system not only to deal with what we find wrong, but also as positive reinforcement. When forms come back, each employee who's favorably mentioned is given some type of recognition or reward. If employees provide good service, Marriott is going to react to that—probably more aggressively than we treat a negative comment.

Once a year we perform a division-wide consumer survey that we've been developing for 15 years. It asks a series of standard questions to compare our services and is conducted by an outside agency that asks a group of consumers how they perceive Marriott, in relation to our competitors, in different aspects of our operation. This gives us a fairly impartial reading of how the consumer feels about us, and how we stand in certain specific areas. Because the survey is repeated annually, we get a good sense of where we're gaining or losing and what we need to emphasize. We also use it to look for those subtle changes in what the customer wants as part of the service. As the industry changes, as needs and travel patterns change, what we must provide to achieve unparalleled standards and exceptional service also changes.

Quality—The USA TODAY Way

Charles R. Blevins
Vice President, Production
Gannett Company, Inc.

USA TODAY was launched on September 15, 1982. In just five years, it has gone from a dream of Gannett's Chairman, Al Neuharth, to the nation's newest tradition for millions of readers and a strong influence on newspapers of the 1980s. USA TODAY's print and color quality has set new industry standards, and we believe that it's our Quality System that enables us to maintain those standards.

Gannett in Perspective

Gannett is a nationwide information company that publishes 90 daily newspapers, including USA TODAY; 35 non-daily newspapers; and USA WEEKEND, a newspaper magazine. It operates 10 television stations, 16 radio stations, and the largest outdoor advertising company in North America. Gannett also has marketing, television news and program production, research, satellite information systems, and a national group of commercial printing facilities. Presently, USA TODAY has 30 domestic print sites with 32 presses, in addition to print sites in Singapore and Switzerland. Plans were recently announced for four more print sites, to be located in St. Louis, Atlanta, Salt Lake City, and Hong Kong.

USA TODAY'S circulation reached 1,600,000 this year, which makes us the second largest daily newspaper in the United States. The USA TODAY International Edition is available in more than 50 countries. Each domestic issue has a maximum of 56 pages, with 16 four-color pages, 11 of which are full-color advertising. About 370 reporters, editors, and researchers write and edit copy on 325 computer terminals at USA TODAY headquarters in Arlington, Virginia. The main computer processes copy and transmits it to phototypesetters. Pages are pasted up and then photographed to create full-page glossy prints. A laser scanner converts the page into electronic signals and an antenna on our building transmits the signal to a satellite.

In three and one-half minutes a black-and-white page is transmitted to the satellite and to all print sites, but it takes up to 10 minutes for each of four separations for a full-color ad, or 40 minutes for the complete color set. Four printing plates are necessary for each color page—blue, red, yellow, and black. Therefore, every color page involves 128 printing plates on 32 presses being in exactly the same position for perfect color registration.

To get back to the production flow, the earth station at each print site receives the signal and sends it to a computer, which converts the electronic signal to an impulse that controls a laser beam that exposes film and produces a full-page negative. The negative is processed and an offset printing plate is produced. USA TODAY presses print copies at an average rate of 18,000 per hour. The newspapers are delivered by truck to approximately 118,000 newsracks, approximately half a million homes, and 80,000 other sales points. USA TODAY has a domestic first edition press start for all sites at 11:45 p.m. and a second edition start of 2:15 a.m.

Meeting the Competition

As we approach the end of the 20th Century, we may be tempted to look back to days that, in our mind's eye, were simpler and less demanding. The driving force for our industry throughout history has been the belief that we would succeed and be competitive because we were needed, because we provided a commodity—news. But, in fact, the newspaper industry is being challenged by many alternative media. Our challenge is to explore and develop creative solutions to the demands of our readers and our advertisers while maintaining stringent cost controls. Our real competition now—which includes television—would like us to meet the same fate as Detroit's automakers.

Color Quality

Rather than ignoring our competition, we have attempted to learn from it, adapting the things that they do well and adding some twists of our own to create a totally new identity. At Gannett and USA TODAY, quality and color are an integral part of this new identity. Color provides the most obvious break with the past and the clearest link to the future, but only if the results reflect the highest quality attainable.

We had a clear mandate from Al Neuharth to do what was considered impossible by most industry experts. He wanted constant, consistent color reproduction across the country—and high quality. The key to our success was and continues to be the total commitment of our senior management to the concept of quality. The core of our strategy was the belief that printing, or as we looked at it, the manufacturing of newspapers, was not a series of independent craft activities, but a system of computers. A system that analyzed cause and effect relationships, looked to vendors for active participation, and, hopefully, allowed people to operate with maximum effectiveness.

We started with some classic tools of quality and manufacturing analysis, research and process capability studies, and many unanswered questions. Rochester Institute of Technology provided us with assistance and counseling in our research efforts. Our friends there designed process capability tests and we provided the testing grounds. The resulting test information and the underlying concepts made us believers in "statistical quality control."

Our foundation is built on the belief that the press has to be a standard for control. A typical offset press operates over a wide range of conditions and still prints a product. This requires the printing process to be right before we start. Advertisers will not pay for poorly reproduced ads. Once printed, there is no room for corrections. So we took steps to standardize press mechanical settings and press operating systems.

Our pre-launch teams spent many hours implementing this project. Much of this effort was devoted to training and retraining people. Even the presses are different. We utilize five different press types from four manufacturers. Because of this diversity, we had to design systems and standards that were general in nature, but that provided enough specific information to be effective. To ensure that the project stays within tolerance, USA TODAY audits each plant a minimum of once each year, more often if needed. The system works because our people work at it.

The key position we created as the result of both our research and training efforts was that of USA TODAY production coordinator. We staffed this position with young graduates from Rochester Institute of Technology in the belief that they would enter our business with few, if any, preconceived ideas about what can and cannot be accomplished. That concept has reaped many benefits, both for Gannett and USA TODAY. Today, some of those first production coordinators are production directors of several Gannett newspapers; others are assistant directors. In addition to RIT, today's production coordinators come from Arizona State University, West Virginia Institute of Technology, California Poly Tech, and Carnegie-Mellon.

Maintaining Standards

Day to day with USA TODAY is like a trip into the future. It is an operation built on the premise that all things are possible. It's space-age from top to bottom. Facsimile systems have advanced to the point where their reliability and quality capabilities make remote publishing a fact of life rather than a dangerous gamble. The operation and control of our network is an excercise in timing and teamwork on a scale comparable to an FAA Control Center. Each day we follow an elaborate testing routine to verify that all facsimile components at every site are operating within tolerance. This includes the actual transmission of test patterns to verify densities and half-tone values.

Although our rate card sets forth clear specifications for USA TODAY advertising materials, a great deal of what we receive is still identical to the material prepared for magazine insertions. About 80 percent of our advertising materials must be remanufactured prior to insertion to correct for size and gradation differences. Every print site has a pre-run and post-run checklist for every piece of equipment. These checklists are used to ensure that elements critical to the process meet standards. Everyone participates in the quality program, even in the mail room or distribution center. That staff inspects papers for accuracy of bundle count, misregister of color, obvious ink imbalances, and other major defects.

Our Quality Assurance Program was designed to provide national advertisers with far better quality than conventional newspapers offered. In a typical press, newsprint moves through the rollers at about 45 miles per hour. As it does, the width of the paper stretches, and different parts of the paper may absorb ink and water at different rates, while moving at high speed. This means great care must be used to get a yellow dot on one plate to line up with a magenta or red dot on another plate. If dots are off a fraction of an inch, the image is a muddy mess. Therefore, all print sites are expected to follow quality guidelines listed in the USA TODAY Standard Operating Procedures manual.

As we all know, you cannot control what you cannot measure. Our Quality Assurance Group rates the print site's papers against our quality standards. Before USA TODAY, newspapers had never tried to use raw materials that met the same specifications every day. The quality of newsprint, of ink, even of the water mixed with ink, varied widely from city to city and from day to day. And newspaper presses were never designed for this level of precision, for full color printed on deadline. National advertisers were used to the standards set by glossy magazines. Newspapers had never tried to match that high standard before. Many advertisers did not believe newspapers could print magazine quality color. Neither did many newspaper publishers, commercial printers, or our suppliers. But Gannett said it was going to do it. And we did.

To address some of the advertisers' concerns with newspapers in general, the subcommittee I chair, for the American Newspaper Publishers Association, recently released "A Guide to Quality Newspaper Reproduction." This was designed to suggest standards for the advertising agencies and newspapers for material and printing. We also recently published a quality guide titled ANPA-Check. This is a checklist of quality elements that influence reader and advertiser perception of newspapers. Once again, a printing plant cannot control what it cannot measure and this applies to evaluating color. We need guidelines because the human eye is not a good, consistent judge of color quality.

When we set out to print USA TODAY, we had no idea that it would affect the rest of the industry. We were just trying to fulfill the editorial and business mission of making the paper as appealing as possible to the widest possible audience. Although we have come far in the last five years, we are constantly challenging ourselves to do better. We are better equipped than ever before to stretch our own limits.

Part VII
Suppliers as Partners

The Xerox Vendor Participation Program

Robert L. Fletcher
Manager, Materials Quality Assurance
Xerox Corporation

Xerox has developed a very close relationship with its suppliers for a simple reason. Of the total per unit manufacturing cost of our copiers, duplicators, and printers, 80 percent is tied up in parts and materials brought from suppliers. In fact, Xerox buys $2 billion worth of productive material a year from its worldwide supplier base. By the late 1970s and early 1980s, we realized we needed to upgrade our operations in order to close the gap between ourselves and our sister company, Fuji Xerox. To lower unit manufacturing costs we had to trim material costs.

In 1981, we formed "commodity teams" for 15 major commodities—such as plastic, sheet metal, and turnings—and we staffed those organizations with design, manufacturing, and quality engineers; product cost staff; and development and procurement people. The goal for each team was to formulate a strategy that would optimize the performance of each commodity in terms of quality, cost, and delivery.

In 1981, we also decided to change our relationship with the 2,000 to 5,000 suppliers we'd been working with, so we narrowed that base down to the best 350. That did not mean we immediately stopped doing business with the remainder, but we focused all new product purchasing on the 350. And, we wanted to reduce that group even further to make them our model suppliers—an extension of Xerox. We started to devote considerable time to training them in statistical process control, just-in-time manufacturing, cooperative costing, set-up time reduction, and supplier involvement.

We wanted to move to an environment in which we could ship directly from the supplier to any manufacturing site or distribution center throughout the world. Our traditional product control technique involved first-piece inspection, manufacturing, and final inspection (see Chart 1). Some of the product goes back to sort and rework, some of it goes to the customer, and a portion of that goes back. Eventually, one can target what's left for customer use—all in all, a very costly operation.

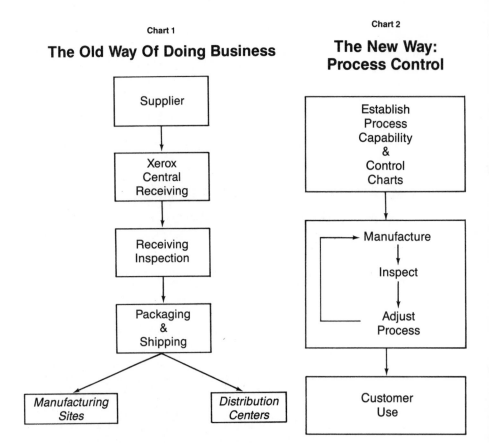

Chart 1

The Old Way Of Doing Business

Chart 2

The New Way: Process Control

The alternative that we wanted to put in place for the 1980s was statistical process control (see Chart 2). We would train our suppliers to establish the necessary process capability and control charts. Then, as they manufactured the product, they could pull samples, compare them to the control chart limits, and adjust the process as needed. The product would be sent directly to the customer.

In 1981, we held a one-day symposium for the chief executive officers or presidents of the 350 suppliers and told them, in short, that every part that came into Xerox from that day forward had to be produced by the process control technique. This would mean eliminating the use of lot acceptance rates and other measures. We wanted 0 percent defect, and 100 percent quality. We also explained there would be a role for them in the development of new Xerox products. Finally, the participants were requested to send their quality production and engineering managers to us for a two- to three-day training program in statistical process control.

By end-1981, and about $500,000 later, we had 33 parts certified by statistical process control. At end-1982, we had about a thousand, and today we have over 20,000. The benefits have been outstanding. In 1981-1982 we measured material quality in terms of lot acceptance. Then we changed over to the system of parts per million and estimated our fallout at 20,000 per million in 1981. In 1982, when we cut the measurement, we were at 10,000 parts per million.

We also developed a benchmarking process. On one side of a Xerox plant, we produced a product designed in the United States and comprised mostly of U.S.-made parts. One the other side of the plant we manufactured a small-volume product that was totally designed by Fuji Xerox. All the components came directly from Japanese suppliers and their benchmark was 950 per million. By end-1986, in less than five years, we went from our original benchmark of 10,000 parts per million fallout to 950 per million. We're looking to be at 125 parts per million fallout by 1989 (see Chart 3). Our manufacturing plants in the United States, Canada, Holland, and England currently have 350 parts per million fallout.

Our ultimate goal was to send material directly from the supplier to Xerox manufacturing sites or distribution centers around the world. When we started in 1981, only 30 percent of the lots from our suppliers went directly to our manufacturing sites or distribution centers. Now over 95 percent of all materials leaving suppliers go directly to those locations.

Xerox's new supplier policies have had other benefits. In 1981, we had 437 people running this material quality organization, in receiving and supplier quality; we now have about 135 people. In 1981, it cost $30 million to run the material quality organization (in 1986 dollars); that's down to about $14 million now.

Chart 3

Purchased Parts Quality
Parts Per Million Line Fallout

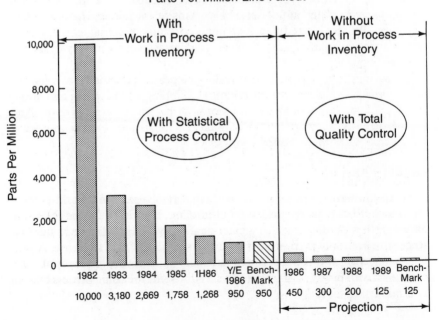

	1982	1983	1984	1985	1H86	Y/E 1986	Bench-Mark	1986	1987	1988	1989	Bench-Mark
	10,000	3,180	2,669	1,758	1,268	950	950	450	300	200	125	125

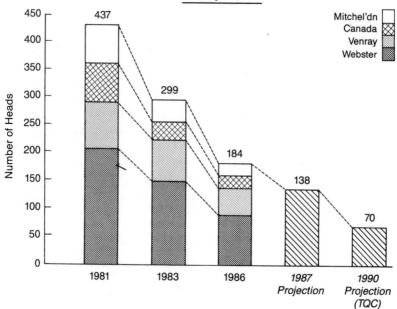

Chart 4

Materials Quality Assurance Manpower

By investing in prevention, we automatically reduced the amount of time spent on failures and appraisals (see Chart 4). In the past, half our time was spent on appraisals—receiving or source inspection. Because those were not effective, we spent the other half of our time working on the failures that the system generated. We also wasted time with nonconforming material, corrective action at suppliers, and purging of parts. In contrast, we spent very little time on prevention.

The savings in my organization alone were peanuts compared to what the new approach would save the corporation. Shipping and handling and inventory reductions save a tremendous amount of money in carrying costs. And the opportunity for more factory automation, better part quality, and fewer line interruptions mean added savings.

Looking Ahead

Xerox now wants to move from a world of certified parts to a world of certified suppliers and that means less hand-holding. The vision for the 1990s is to have suppliers produce parts at greater quality levels. Initially, we found that some suppliers only used process control on products sold to Xerox. A year later we discovered that many of our suppliers were moving to supply all their customers with process control products. Now some are using process control as a marketing tool.

90

We will also foster the concept of constant improvement. When we talk about total quality to our suppliers, we urge them to build their prime business strategy around management attitudes, practices, and behaviors that foster quality. In the year ahead, we will be working with our suppliers in the following areas:

- *Focusing on the customer.* Suppliers should think in terms of internal and external customer requirements.
- *Benchmarking.* We want to teach our suppliers to establish benchmarks for every aspect of their businesses, as Xerox has.
- *Reducing the cost of quality by half.* This would be a tremendous opportunity both for the supplier and for Xerox. We're spending $2 billion a year in material purchases from our suppliers. If cost of quality amounts to 20 percent or 30 percent that means at least $400 million can be saved.
- *Problem solving.* We will pass on the tools we learned at Xerox— including a six-step problem-solving tool and a nine-step quality-improvement tool. And, we're developing a technique for the design of experiments.
- *Total quality orientation.* Finally, we want to give total quality orientation to CEOs and champions within supplier organizations who will carry this process beyond the core group. We plan to do that in four phases:

(1) A commodity team manager will call together ten supplier CEOs for a two-day seminar to explain Xerox's Leadership through Quality Program and the concept of total quality.

(2) We will prepare CEOs to lead their senior staff members through three days of training on the concept of total quality.

(3) The CEOs and their senior staff will spend 60 to 90 hours together formulating their mission statement and discussing how to implement quality policy in their companies.

(4) The supplier firms will educate all of their employees in the total quality process.

We believe it's going to take us two years to get through 100 suppliers, 60 in North America and 40 in Europe. We've already got 20 suppliers as far as steps two and four. Most of our suppliers are of a size—about 200 employees—that we consider conducive to cultural change.

Nylomold: A Case Study

John S. Vangellow
President and Chief Executive Officer
Nylomold Corporation

I represent a supplier firm that's already gone through Xerox's program. There are several team objectives in working with Xerox. Both parties, with the investment Xerox is making in us and that we are making ourselves, are looking for a fair return on investment. We're looking for a long-term commitment for quality of product and for improved delivery time. The total quality concept, as we see it in partnership with Xerox or any of our other customers, will lead to becoming a world-class supplier for all of our customers.

Nylomold is a custom injection-molding business and assembly operation located in Rochester, New York. We have 125 employees, 38,000 square feet, and have broken ground for a 22,000 square-foot addition. Our company uses 40 injection-molding machines, microprocessor controls, robotic systems, and a shuttle injection-molding system. From 1983 through 1985, Xerox introduced us to statistical-process control. Nylomold worked directly with their supplier quality assurance and part certification programs and they gave us direct in-house assistance. We started early supplier involvement and supplier networking—in other words, using certified suppliers that had gone through the same Xerox program we had.

What are some of the benefits of our association with Xerox?

- The first tangible result was a reduction in part failures and rejection rate. We reached the level of 100 parts per million rejection, which is lower than the Xerox goal, and as low as the Japanese record at that time.
- Our on-time delivery rate is now 98 percent. This improvement was especially rapid—virtually overnight.
- We've reduced or eliminated inspections of incoming parts.
- We've received awards for excellence from Xerox, Eastman Kodak, IBM, and NCR.
- We have reduced our base of suppliers, as Xerox did.
- With early supplier involvement, we reduced our lead time and manufacturing costs dramatically.

One way we reduced cost was by working with Xerox engineers to establish a target cost. Together we reviewed specs and determined the best materials to be used. Our joint system for establishing product cost ensures that both parties get a fair return and share in the savings we achieve by working together.

In 1986-1987, we introduced training in and implementation of just-in-time manufacturing. (Some of the employees thought, "Well, we're there already. We really get our parts out the door just in time.") Xerox representatives spent 16 hours talking to two groups of our employees (about 45 employees in each group). Their engineering support has been available to us in areas like mold-flow analysis, CAD/CAM, and robotic systems. We've also had the opportunity to participate in international supplier seminars in Japan and Europe and have been a part of reciprocating visits by Japanese and Chinese groups. The opportunity to meet with European suppliers and to observe Xerox operations in Europe may lead to significant cross-fertilization.

Our newest program is a direct computer link with order-entry accounting at Xerox. Next will come a direct-payment program linked via computer, which will affect cash flow, which is very important in small companies. Finally, Xerox has exposed us to leadership through quality, which ties all these just-in-time manufacturing programs together. Here's an overview of some results achieved from the just-in-time process:

- A 12 to 15 percent reduction in machine time rates per hour,
- A 75 percent reduction in machine setup costs and cycle time,
- Reduction in machine rates to customers,
- Work cell concept in use,
- Lowering of part lead times,
- Improved delivery performance,
- Reduction in inventories,
- More efficient space utilization,
- Delivery direct to all customer manufacturing sites.

And, since we've become involved in the total quality program, for the first time in our history, we have a company mission statement, quality policy, and vision of the future (see Box).

Elements of EPQ

Nylomold now has its own quality program, called Excellence, the Power of Quality (EPQ), a phrase and acronym developed by our employees. EPQ has seven elements, which were developed by our senior staff and senior management:

(1) *Management behaviors:* Dedicated to supporting and emulating the desired behaviors of EPQ and total commitment to EPQ.

(2) *Quality principles:* Management's quality philosophy communicated throughout the company by quality policy, quality practices, strategic vision (mission and goals). Plans are developed and implemented to achieve employee involvement in all areas of the business. Plans are developed and implemented for quality training, communications, reward, and recognition.

Nylomold Corporation

Company Mission Statement

Nylomold, as a progressive and dedicated team of employees in the custom injection-molding business, offers complete design, manufacture, and assembly of precision plastic products. As a company, we recognize the need for quality precision products in world markets and in support of these requirements fully utilize our resources to achieve employee enrichment and total customer value while striving for a fair return on investment.

Company Quality Policy

Since its inception in 1962, Nylomold has built its reputation and success through a commitment to total quality as the basis for meeting customer requirements. Through our responsible employees, we are able to offer consistency, excellent service, and support to all our customers. Employing state-of-the-art technology and continuous quality-assurance processes makes Nylomold's primary objective of zero defects obtainable.

Vision of the Future

Through the implementation of total quality concepts, we will grow in market share, diversification of product and service, employee enrichment, and above all, customer value. Quality will be a continual course of action and will become part of the fiber of each employee, customer, and supplier. All those associated with Nylomold will realize *excellence through quality.*

(3) *Competitive benchmarking:* A continuous process of *measuring* our parts, services, prices and practices against our competitors or those companies who are the best in their business.

(4) *Cost of quality:* A systematic process for determining the cost of quality. Opportunities to reduce the cost of quality are prioritized and pursued through employee-involvement and quality-improvement processes.

(5) *Customer relationships:* Giving customers what they require in order to meet their satisfaction; specifications are developed for each of their requirements. With this form of work process, customer satisfaction can be achieved.

(6) *Problem-solving process:* A systematic road map used by individuals and teams to identify and remove barriers to quality. It allows employees to be creative and gives them a voice in the company's development.

(7) *Quality technologies:* Statistical quality control, measurement, and manufacturing engineering technologies utilized to achieve competitive benchmarks, reduce cost of quality, and fully satisfy customer requirements.

SMCL
658.5 Sch25   stack
/Total quality performance : highlights

3 5151 00017 0175